COPING

WITH

Difficult

Teachers

Gary Bergreen

THE ROSEN PUBLISHING GROUP, INC./NEW YORK

Published in 1988 by The Rosen Publishing Group, Inc.
29 East 21st Street, New York, NY 10010

First Edition

LIBRARY OF CONGRESS
Library of Congress Cataloging-in-Publication Data

Bergreen, Gary.
   Coping with difficult teachers / Gary Bergreen. — 1st ed.
     p.   cm.
   Includes index.
   ISBN 0-8239-0788-0
   1. Teacher-student relationships. 2. Teachers-Attitudes. 3.
Student adjustment. I. Title
LB1033.B475 1988
371.1'02—dc19   88-20107
                                            CIP
                                            AC

Manufactured in U.S.A.

Fellowship with Man

But when two people are at one in their inmost hearts,

They shatter even the strength of iron or of bronze.

And when two people understand each other in their inmost hearts,

Their words are sweet and strong, like the fragrance of orchids.

I CHING
or Book of Changes
(c. twelfth century B.C.)

Contents

Preface

The way you feel about yourself and your teachers is very important if you want to become a winner. Dealing with difficult teachers with who you must come into contact daily is certainly no easy task.

Teachers and students see school from different perspectives. As a student, you try to survive the day-to-day, hour-by-hour routine of classroom existence, a restricting way of life that has its good moments and its bad moments.

For students, school means sitting on hard chairs at uncomfortable desks, listening and maybe daydreaming, reading, writing, and staying out of serious trouble.

For teachers, school means a week-to-week, semester-by-semester challenge to educate students who may or may not even want to be educated. They interact with thirty-five students during six or seven fifty-minute periods, five days a week. Communication is continuous, often exhausting, and sometimes ineffective because, more often than not, it is laced with angry reprimands and defensive remarks and accusations.

Yet everyone tries to get through the school day with minimal interpersonal conflict. Some school relationships even turn out to be both enjoyable and stimulating. There are always, however, a few teachers who are difficult to get along with; they seem to pop up in the classes you discover you dislike the most.

Teachers are in the human relations business. They have gone to college and received a degree and teaching credentials. The state has certified them as bona fide, capable teachers. Distressingly, their ability to be caring, sympathetic human beings is frequently overlooked and all too often questionable.

Teachers become teachers usually because they care about the needs and aspirations of young people, and they work toward establishing a friendly, positive relationship with them. But those few difficult teachers who expect too much from their students seem to possess little patience or empathy when students act like students—insensitive, impulsive, argumentative, and curious.

Schools bring strangers together. Students from all types of backgrounds must somehow cope with one another, learn from one another, and share experiences with one another. Teachers use their authority to instruct them and to probe, demand, and dictate to them. Students in turn learn, whimper, argue, and challenge this authority. Some teachers don't really care to teach; some students don't really care to learn. Some make excuses for their failures and begin to hate school. Others can't or won't cope with people, rules, or school at all. They also have difficulty coping with frustration, tension, and hostility created by a poor teacher-student relationship.

So you need to know where you stand in relationship to the expectations of others. Next, you must decide what strategies and techniques are best for you in overcoming difficult school situations and personal crises. And finally, you need to practice being a winner a little more often, to take charge of your own emotions and resolve conflicts more successfully.

What should you do when you meet a difficult teacher? What are your alternatives? What strategies will help you stay out of trouble and at the same time give you more opportunities to be a winner and enjoy school more?

The aim of this book is to answer those and other questions as well as to help you (1) discover why students and teachers act the way they do toward each other, (2) understand how to take charge of those mixed emotions that usually contribute to unstable relationships, (3) cope with difficult situations and teachers, and (4) gain a more positive attitude toward yourself and a clearer perspective of life. Also included are the candid, uninhibited thoughts and feeling of students at the secondary level.

CHAPTER 1

Students Talk Back

SAYS SHARON:

> Who am I? I'm just an average, healthy girl, a person of many interests. I consider myself active and fairly smart, but I could probably do better in my schoolwork if I studied a little harder.

Sound familiar? Such sentiments are expressed by students in junior and senior high school. You may be one of those who have a positive attitude toward themselves and others. You may be among those who are satisfied with going to school, getting good grades, and meeting new friends.

FINDING YOURSELF IN THE CROWD

SAYS MARK:

> Sometimes I wonder about myself. I have trouble making friends because it seems like people are always picking on me. I can't help it if I'm so sensitive.

It's just the way I am. And this makes me really unhappy because it means so much to me to have friends.

Some students have more problems than they can handle. They don't seem to get along with anyone. School is a nightmare to them. Their feelings of dread and frustration go unchecked, growing more intense with each passing class. These students get poor grades, lack interest, have few friends, have a low opinion of themselves; to them, life seems meaningless.

SAYS PETE:

People think I'm happy because I'm so loud all the time, but the truth of the matter is that I'm very self-conscious about so many things, and I hope no one ever finds this out. I would die of embarrassment.

Sometimes the way you see yourself affects how you act around others. Feeling good about yourself helps you feel good about those around you.

SAYS ANNA:

It just doesn't seem fair. My teachers expect me to understand these really difficult concepts, yet my parents still treat me like a child, by making me go to bed early.

Trying to find out who you are and what you stand for in this ever-changing world is indeed difficult to do. And as you have already found out by now, difficult teachers don't make matters any easier.

WHY ME?

SAYS RANDY:

Growing up is really difficult. I'm always changing my mind about something, even from one day to the next. I won't deny the fact that I'm very influenced by my friends. I just can't help it.

When we're young, responsibilities seem overwhelming. And many questions are without answers. For example: Why are teachers so difficult? Why is school so hard? Shouldn't I be getting a little more fun out of life? What's ahead for me anyway?

SAYS JOHN:

When I get a failing mark on a test, I get so angry at my teacher, that I really wish I could give her a piece of my mind. I know I probably deserved that grade, but I resent it anyway.

Life is full of questions and responsibilities. When we can't cope with them, we blame others. That's one reason why some students sit in class and wonder: "Why me? Why is this teacher always picking on me?"

The questions asked and the demands teachers make can really ruin your day. What is it about school that really bothers you? Boring classes? Mean teachers? Homework? During those bad days it may seem as if all your teachers want to know where your homework is, what happened to your textbook, and on and on.

DIGGING YOURSELF OUT OF DIFFICULTIES

Some students know exactly what they want out of life. They know early on that they want to become astronauts, scientists, engineers, or entertainers. And they also know that they must make some sacrifices—spending extra time practicing and studying, and doing whatever is necessary to reach their career goals.

Coping with difficult teachers is one of the roadblocks that students must face while still keeping their goals in focus.

SAYS CRAIG:

> I would like to be independent. I don't like it when I have to ask someone for a favor. I don't really want to be famous. All I want is a good job and lots of friends.

Getting what you want is one of life's great challenges. Many people are unable to satisfy their needs because they keep beating their heads against a wall. They look in the wrong places for solutions to their problems.

But some problems don't go away until you do something about them. How do you do that?

Well, digging out the right answers is a lot like prospecting for gold. And like a prospector, you need to (1) know where to look, (2) have the right tools, and (3) have the patience of a gold miner!

Where to Look

Teachers do not always have the all right answers, and neither do the textbooks. But they're an excellent place to start. And don't depend too much on your friends to solve your problems because they might be going through the same stage right now. So where else can you look? There is another place, deep down inside yourself.

Your own brain can be an untapped source of wealth. It holds every experience you have ever had and every idea you have ever thought. You have the ability to discover many of the answers you are seeking. But like a prospector, you must dig deep for the solutions.

The Digging Tools

You also need the right tools to solve your problems and cope with difficult teachers and school situations. Those tools include clear thinking, an ability to adapt to difficult situations, and a positive attitude.

Patience

You need patience and also the ability to communicate effectively with others. It is vital to develop and sharpen your communication skills (speaking, listening, writing, and reading). They will help you to shape and devise new strategies, to see old ideas in unique ways, and to see what you may not want to see through the eyes of other people.

Being patient will help you get through those bad days. People will be less difficult. So by knowing where to look and what tools to use, and by having a little patience, you can understand people better and bring about a more positive working relationship with them. And that's where the richest vein of gold is really hidden, as you will soon discover.

STRIKE IT RICH WITH SELF-CONFIDENCE

According to the old adage, there is more than one way to skin a cat. Also, to solve a problem, handle a teacher, or reach your goal. But first, to cope with the business of school, you must learn to stay ahead of the game. How? By being confident in yourself, by feeling that you are, indeed, a worthwhile person. When you're in school and teachers, parents, and friends are making you feel worthless, say to yourself, "Each day I am becoming both a little older and a little better able to handle problems that come my way." Remember, the right answers must come first from you, from deep within, and then from school. School is a good place to learn about yourself. Many students, in fact, see school not as a place to run from, but as a place to walk slowly through.

SAYS MAXINE:

> I like myself because I think I have a pretty good personality and get along well with people, except for some of my teachers. That's a different story entirely.

Discovering those golden nuggets of knowledge, though, takes knowing where to look, knowing how to use your brain, and having a little ingenuity and a lot of patience. Here, very little luck is involved in being a winner and striking it rich.

COPING WITH SCHOOL PROBLEMS

SAYS SAL:

> I'm a straight A student. But besides getting good

grades, I think I'm pretty good at understanding what makes people do the things they do.

Frustration, tension, and anxiety sometimes seem to be what school is all about. You're afraid to talk to your teachers. You're under pressure to finish an assignment or pass a test. Or you're getting upset and making others mad at you, especially teachers who want you to do things you don't want to do. You want to learn but you just don't know how. So you fight back by grumbling, complaining, and criticizing. If this sounds like you, stop! There are more effective ways of coping with school life.

SAYS CONNIE:

School is really a drag. I hate the teachers who are always giving us a lot of homework to do.

SAYS JIM:

Maybe I'm too critical, but I just can't seem to respect teachers who are too strict or who are just plain boring or who can't control their students. These kinds of teachers shouldn't be allowed in classrooms.

SAYS EDITH:

I just can't stand it when teachers are shorter than me. I get so embarrassed when I'm walking next to them.

SAYS CARMEN:

I guess maybe we're too hard on teachers. Just look at the students they have to deal with. It's enough to drive anyone crazy. But I'll have to admit one thing —teachers must really like their jobs; they come back every year.

SAYS: _____
      Your name

(Write your own comments on a separate sheet of paper about your experiences in school and your teachers.)

Writing down what you are thinking can be a very good strategy, especially when it comes to figuring out how you really feel about school. Many students keep journals, diaries, and logs of their day-to-day experiences. Here is a way for you to get started with your log entries:

A. Begin each day by writing down one goal.
   - Solve part of a problem.
   - Stay out of trouble.
   - Make a new friend.
   - Get better grades.
   - Do your best.
B. Reread your log at least three times during the day.
   - Remind yourself of your goal.
   - If achieving this goal won't make you a winner, forget it.
C. At the end of each day, write down some additional observations.
   - What happened during the day?
   - Did you meet your goal?
   - How did you feel about the effort you made?

Even if you don't like to do a lot of writing, this strategy is very relaxing, and it takes only a few minutes each day.

And remember, you are the only one who will ever read those daily entries.

Try it for a week. You will discover some very important things about yourself—how you cope with teachers and school and yourself! In addition, you just might find the answer to the question: Where am I trying to go and am I really getting there in good shape?

TRADE-OFF

At this point, you may be hesitating, wondering what would happen if you really did strike gold, if you did find the right answers. Wouldn't your parents just expect more of you? Wouldn't teachers expect you to work harder? Wouldn't you have to meet more demands and cope with more responsibilities? Perhaps.

SAYS MITCH:

> I'm the kind of student who has to study real hard to get good grades. But what's really frustrating is that everyone expects me to keep on getting good grades. That means I have to study and have less time to play basketball, which I'm really good at. And I certainly can't get Cs, since everyone will think I'm just being plain lazy. So either way, I lose!

SAYS JUSTIN:

> You just have to do the best you can, in school, on your job, or when you get married. That's what life is all about.

In school there are decisions and trade-offs to be made. If you decide to invest your time in learning and studying, you will get good grades and chances are, your future will turn out the way you want it to. On the other hand, if you decide to party all the time, to socialize and make a lot of friends at the expense of failing classes and disappointing parents and teachers, you are trading a future that you want for one that you may not want.

Your future needs careful planning. Some students are losers in this respect because they refuse to take charge and be responsible for their own decisions. And making the right decision isn't always easy. In fact, dealing with life is never easy, but it *is* necessary!

Those who are winners make plans, see their mistakes, and devise better strategies to make better decisions. They are the ones who dig for the golden opportunities.

SAYS PAM:

> When something goes wrong, I try to change it, and I think I know the difference between what's right and what's wrong. I know I can do my best and that's important to me. I don't care about what others expect of me; my own expectations are what count.

COPING BY ADAPTING

In school, when the going gets tough, deciding what you should do next can seem to be next to impossible. The trick is to stay in control of your emotions, to develop a take-charge attitude, and to turn school problems into Win-Win Situations, ones where everyone compromises and comes out a winner. That means that you must learn to adapt to situations by being more objective. Be calm and friendly. It's a good way to maintain a close working relationship with difficult teachers.

We all have our days. So your job is to adapt to the way people act from one minute to the next. Observe their moods and anticipate their needs as well as their demands on you. If you don't learn to cope, you will find that difficult people will only upset you and keep you off balance. To adapt to difficult people is not very difficult. Have a take-charge attitude and a sense of worth, and be calm under pressure.

> RULE 1. CHANGE YOUR BEHAVIOR. THEN ADJUST TO DAILY SCHOOL PROB- LEMS WITH CONFIDENCE AND A TAKE-CHARGE ATTITUDE.

Thinking negative thoughts about yourself, your teachers, and school is really self-defeating. It can become a habit, one that consumes your every waking minute. Instead, take charge of your emotions, think positively, and look for the best in others.

If your teachers become a big problem, you need effective strategies to cope with them. Here's an easy way to begin. When you get in trouble with a difficult teacher, take a deep breath, count to ten, and instead of being argumentative, become neutral and friendly.

CHAPTER ◦ 2

Students Learning to Cope

SAYS MICHELLE:

> I can't stand school because it's just a waste of time. Why do we have to get up in the morning to come to school? Why not in the afternoon? I also hate school because we have to read out loud for ten minutes every day. Reading is so boring, especially in the morning.

All too often, a classroom can be a combat zone where the battle cry of the teacher, "Sit down and be quiet!" echoes off the wall as loud as any cannon shot.

Teachers spend some twenty-two thousand minutes each school year punishing, reprimanding, nagging, or in some other way trying to control their students. But is that really what education is all about? Is that the kind of place where parents want to send their children every day? Where battle lines are drawn, where there are no learners, only losers? Both teacher and student are dissatisfied. Neither is productive or happy. Both wind up losers. Does this war of words sound familiar?

STUDENT: (waving his hand and jumping up and down in his seat, trying to attract his teacher's attention, who seems to be ignoring him, fed up with his persistent questions)

TEACHER: What is it *now*?

STUDENT: I don't understand this math problem. Could you please explain it?

TEACHER: Well, maybe if you tried doing your homework once in awhile, the lessons wouldn't be that difficult.

STUDENT: Well, it's just a bunch of words and numbers to me. They just don't make any sense. I don't see where learning this is at all relevant to what I want to do when I get out of high school.

(The math teacher, at the end of her patience with students always giving her the same story about how, when they're rich and famous, they will have absolutely no need to have any understanding of math whatsoever, clenches her fists, loses her cool, and storms out of the room, slamming the door behind her.)

An exaggerated example? Well, perhaps. But you have probably witnessed a similar clash of wills, a run-in betweeen student and teacher that stopped just short of flogging!

You may even have found *yourself* on the defensive. You argue; the teacher yells. Both of you wind up in an emotional situation in which you are punished and the teacher's day is ruined. That is what is known as a No-Win Situation: Neither you nor the teacher wins.

Such situations are all too common. They begin and end, more often than not, like the following:

STUDENT: I think I must have left my book home. I can't seem to find it.
(Forgetful or *negligent?)*

TEACHER: What, *again!* Now, would you like to tell me just how you're going to do today's assignment?
(Reprimand)

STUDENT: (to other students): I am really getting fed up with this teacher.
(Put-down)

TEACHER: I heard that! If you don't be quiet, I'm putting you on detention.
(Insult and *threat)*

STUDENT: (ignores the teacher, laughs, and whispers to others)

TEACHER: That's it! I've had it! That's the last straw!
(yelling)　　Down to the principal's office with you —march! And you've got yourself two hours of detention.
(Implementing threat)

HELLO, WORLD!

When teachers lose their cool or overreact to what their students say or do, they lose control of the classroom situation. Why? Because words are exchanged without regard for their possible consequences. In an emotionally charged atmosphere where no one is in control, a No-Win Situation is inevitably created.

Here is another scenario that you might have experienced: You wake up on a typical school morning, and you say to yourself, "I'd rather stay in bed, but OK, I have to get up. So, *hello, world!*"

Now you are up, and you begin to realize, "Hey, I feel pretty good, no aches, no pains, a little hungry, but breakfast will take care of that. I feel good about myself. I'm alert. Everything fits together because there is a place for everything and everything is in its place. I really feel in control!"

Then you go to school and what happens? Bells are ringing, teachers are giving orders, and students keep shouting and slamming into you in the crowded hallway. No matter. You get to class, sit down, and first period is about to begin.

But as you sit in your seat, your world—you know, the one that had everything in place only a few minutes ago—now slowly begins to unravel. The teacher begins playing brain games, asking questions you know you could never possibly answer even if you had done your homework the night before. "I'm surprised you don't know the answer," she says, and everyone's eyes are on you. And the more she talks, the more your nerves come unhinged. She talks about things you have never heard of, using words that don't make any sense. And all you can do is scratch your head, look at the clock, and discover in horror, "It's only 8:20! This is still only first period." Six or seven other teachers are waiting to humiliate you. Your world is slowly turning upside down. *"Hello, world!"*

But then you begin to look on the bright side. You got through school yesterday with a minimum of strain and pain. You read an interesting story, made a little sense out of science, and heard some new ideas that made you curious. And so you listened a little to get the gist of things, long enough so you didn't become too confused. Of course, when you got bored in your last class, you naturally turned your attention to your friends sitting next to you. But that time you got caught for whispering and giggling; better not try that again, unless the teacher isn't looking.

It just depends on how you look at school and how you want to feel about your teachers. You have a right to find the right attitude and right viewpoint, so make the most of them.

From a teacher's point of view, school is perceived as a month-by-month, semester-by-semester sequence of lesson plans, projects, assignments, and learning activities. But students view school differently. They see it almost exclusively as a day-to-day, hour-by-hour bombardment of busywork and tests. Of course, some school activities are more interesting than others: sports events, dances, assemblies, and even some films and discussions, for example.

FINDING COMMON GROUND

SAYS RON:

> The thing I hate about school is that too many teachers are mean, and too many students are nerds! They push you around and think they're hot stuff. They're not cool. They're all a bunch of fools!

Naturally, when students don't see eye to eye with teachers, conflicts arise and students become more and more frustrated with school and with the entire learning process. But some students handle tough situations successfully. They don't always have the right answers, and they don't always make the best decisions; still, they do find ways to cope with difficult teachers.

* * *

For example, take the case of Janet, a ninth grader. She has learned to adapt to difficult teachers. This story was told by Janet's mother, who conferred with her daughter's English teacher. The teacher reported that Janet was doing quite well in the course, and that her behavior was good. His only criticism was that Janet never raised her hand in class.

At home, Janet explained to her mother that whenever she analyzed a story in class, her interpretation never coincided with her teacher's. So she was naturally reluctant to volunteer answers that she knew would be unacceptable. But at the same time, to get the best possible grade, Janet had to adapt her behavior to the teacher's expectations by (1) using self-control; (2) maintaining a take-charge attitude; and (3) giving the desired response on written examinations.

Janet's story is not unusual except perhaps in one respect. She was a very bright student in a special class called "Honors and Leadership," a class where students were expected to be both *honest* and *intelligent*.

RULE 2. NOBODY NEEDS TO FEEL LIKE A FAILURE. THERE ARE SO MANY ALTERNATIVES AND EFFECTIVE STRATEGIES TO RELY ON WHEN COPING WITH DIFFICULT PEOPLE. WHENEVER POSSIBLE, FIND THE WIN-WIN SITUATION.

Teachers may or may not ask an endless barrage of tough questions. But that's not the real problem. The difficulty is that there just isn't enough time to think the question through or to come up with the correct answer.

Research shows that the time between asking a question and expecting a student's response is extremely short. Why? Because most teachers feel uncomfortable waiting for more than *three seconds* in "dead silence." Nothing is happening—supposedly! So the question and answer period becomes very awkward. Students feel tense and with good reason. The teacher actually interferes with the student's thinking process by prodding and rephrasing questions, adding, "Now think! Let me put it to you another way. What if?" In the end, a perplexed student ventures a guess just to relieve the tension of the moment.

SECRETS OF BEING A WINNER

Students who see school as a challenge don't get beaten. By devising better school strategies, you can stay out of trouble, get better grades, and discover many new and fascinating ideas.

A winner is someone who gets what he wants by influencing others. You will know you are a winner in school when you learn to gain approval, praise, sympathy, support, and friendship through effective communication. You will be a winner when you take control of your behavior and become responsible for achieving personal goals. Unfortunately, not everyone knows the secrets of being a winner. Do you?

Secret 1. Establish a working relationship. When you first meet a new teacher, or anyone else for that matter, you begin to establish a relationship, one with a wide range of verbal and nonverbal possibilities. From a variety of possible messages, you and the teacher must select only those words, gestures, and expressions that you both agree are appropriate.

For instance, you can agree on exchanging insults or compliments, praise or negative remarks, or interesting information or hostility and frustration.

In almost every relationship there is an unspoken agreement called a *mutual definition* of terms and expectations. Keep in mind that such an understanding between any two persons is complex and always changing. Everything that is said or done reinforces the understanding or suggests a way to modify that definition, and thus affects the behavior found in that relationship.

If, for example, your teacher puts an arm around you and you shrug it off, you have just indicated that this type of friendly behavior makes you feel uncomfortable.

But remember, it takes two to establish and maintain any working relationship, especially in a classroom on a daily basis. It's not easy either, because relationships never remain the same for very long. The way you and your teacher act toward each other one day may be different the next day.

A responsible teacher makes relationships work to the benefit of all concerned. But beware! Some teachers don't really know how to take control or to resolve class situations. Some teachers may inadvertently be difficult, argumentative, and make snap judgments that you don't like. Teachers, too, are only human. So you need to cope with different kinds of personalities, some friendly, some demanding, and still others strange and confusing.

Some disagreements and conflicts will always exist in your classes. Be aware of them, come to grips with them, and cope with them, using all the strategies that you know. If this fails, you still have other people you can depend on for help—the student adviser, the principal, other teachers, parents, and other family members. They will help you arrange a transfer from one class to another if you find you are unable to resolve a personality conflict with a teacher.

Before you consider that alternative, however, sit down and have a little talk with yourself. Evaluate your own intentions, attitudes, and feelings toward the teacher.

- Is it the teacher or is it I who is being difficult?
- Who really gets angry most often and why?
- By changing my behavior, can I help build a better relationship?

You may not always like the answer, but you will have a clearer understanding of your relationship and you will know just where you stand.

Secret 2. Stay in control of the situation. To be a winner, you must first learn to face difficult people calmly. You can do this by keeping your emotions under control and by thinking before you speak. Yelling and other outbursts of defiance only make you a loser.

Two essential elements of a working relationship that will help you stay in control are *respect* and a *sense of belonging*. Without either of these, communication breaks downs, tempers flare, and learning or coping in class deteriorates to no more than an exercise in futility.

Secret 3. Take charge and look for better alternatives. The secret in resolving personal problems is having the ability to communicate effectively. For instance, when you get involved in an argument with your teacher, practice being calm and stay neutral rather than being argumentative, and be ready to take charge, to discuss better alternatives.

In the classroom there must be *two-way communication*

between you and the teacher. Both of you must listen and respond with empathy, not antagonism, mutual respect, not hostility, with the purpose of finding a Win-Win Situation.

Effective communication means defining, examining, and attempting to resolve conflicts by compromising and agreeing on a better course of action. Effective communication is vital if you are to learn, if the teacher is to teach, and if both of you are to continue an amicable working relationship.

We are all looking for better ways to socialize, to share information, and to express our own wants and desires. Staying in tune with school and with the changes that are going on all around you is one of the greatest challenges you will ever face. Meeting that challenge will help you find better ways to cope.

CHAPTER 3

Mixed Emotions

About School

SAYS FRANCIS:

> School's too emotional. I know the problem is me,
> but the teacher doesn't have to get so upset all the
> time. She knew I had to take my medication. At
> times she's pretty nice and has a sense of humor. But
> she's always telling me to sit down; it just gets on my
> nerves. I guess teachers have to be strict, but why do
> they have to be mean? They should be fair but not get
> people mad or frustrated.

Our emotions play a significant role in our lives. We feel
good about certain kinds of music, movies, sports, and
food. We feel bad about illness, death, poverty, and
disease. At school we react emotionally toward the students and teachers in class, toward the assignment, and
toward homework we are expected to do. Sometimes there
seems to be more in school to dislike than like.

Students react negatively to teachers they don't like. In fact, they give up trying and get failing grades, not because they aren't intelligent, but because there is no working relationship between teachers and students.

SAYS WALTER:

> It makes me very nervous to count to one hundred. I can't stand it when the teacher stares at me and I fall apart when she yells at me when I make mistakes. My stomach gets butterflies and I sweat a lot. It's the same in my other classes.

The more pressure a teacher puts on students, the more the students tend to feel mad, upset, or complain of physical discomfort. They are sending subtle signals to the teacher that they are trying to cope with mixed emotions such as tension, frustration, hostility, and even depression.

Do you stay in control of your emotions while you are in school? Many of your friends hide their emotions. A few are unable to deal with emotional situations in class; they become defensive or angry and throw temper tantrums. Most students become frustrated when their school day is filled with an excessive amount of demands, reprimands, and negative communication. That is when they distance themselves as much as possible from the learning process, the classroom, and the entire school setting.

Do you lose control when teachers get mad at you? Treat you unfairly? Ignore you? If you do, you can count yourself among the notorious group that has been multilabeled dunces, misfits, incorrigibles, disciplinary problems, and slow learners.

Very important is the way you act in school, the way you control your emotions. It takes conscious effort as well as strategies and social skills to be able to cope with difficult teachers and school encounters. Emotions are hard to handle, especially for students maturing into adulthood.

The point is that you are likely to cope successfully with difficult people only after you understand your own feelings and how they affect a working relationship. By understanding yourself a little better, you will have a much better chance of turning out to be a winner in difficult school encounters.

UNDERSTANDING ME BETTER

How would you describe the way others see you? Likable? Friendly? Good-natured? A loner? Cold? Untrustworthy? You are many different people all rolled up in one body. You are someone's child, friend, enemy, student, relative, consumer, and employee. You are loved, respected, tolerated, and hated. Still you *are* you, no matter what others may think.

Following is a list of words that describe personality traits that some people might see in you. Make a check mark to indicate which words accurately describe who you are nearly always, sometimes, or never.

WHO AM I, REALLY?

	Nearly always	Sometimes	Never
Cooperative	———	———	———
Friendly	———	———	———
Frustrated	———	———	———
Loud	———	———	———
Irritable	———	———	———
Intelligent	———	———	———
Withdrawn	———	———	———
Disorganized	———	———	———

Good-natured			
Sloppy			
Depressed			
Energetic			
Prejudiced			
Open-minded			
Talkative			
Funny			
Serious			
Hostile			
Confident			

Take a few minutes to review your choices. On another piece of paper, write down everything you know about yourself, your good qualities and your bad qualities.

If you are to cope with difficult teachers, you must first believe in yourself and in your ability to devise strategies that will help you take control of school situations. You must anticipate difficult situations and know what to do about them. These questions will help you gain some insight into how you perceive yourself and others in school.

- Can I adjust my behavior when faced with difficult situations?
- Do I really care about myself and what I am able to accomplish in school?
- Do I really care about what others think of me?
- Can I learn to talk with my teachers without feeling embarrassed or threatened?
- Do teachers take time to understand me?

Here is an easy strategy to try the next time you are in a classroom with a difficult teacher. Some students have an amazing ability to detect the kind of mood a teacher is in and adjust to it accordingly. The way to do that is by observing the teacher's posture, facial expressions, mannerisms, and tone of voice, subtle clues that will alert you to how much that teacher is willing to put up with and what the breaking point is that day. Many students pick up these clues early in the semester so that they know just how quiet or talkative they can be, what to say and what not to say, and when and how to answer questions.

PLAN AHEAD

Due dates and deadlines! It seems as if every teacher is telling you there is a deadline for turning in your work, finishing a test, or completing a class project. And the closer you come to that deadline, the more uneasy you feel. If you don't plan ahead and take charge of your future, you will continue to experience frustration and anxiety. You don't need that aggravation if you can help it. *And you can help it!*

Does this sound like a typical school crisis? Your English teacher has just assigned a book report to be completed over the weekend. Or your science teacher wants you to finish your Science Fair project no later than Monday morning—*no later!*

Hey, no problem! You understand the assignment. You have plenty of time to complete the work. You know you can finish it within the next seventy-two hours. No hurry. No need to plan ahead. So you set all thoughts of school aside until...

You begin working on the assignment Sunday evening around eight o'clock and you work through the wee morning hours. It turns out to be a little more work than you planned on. Anyway, you finally finish, and the assignment is all ready to be turned in.

Monday morning. The alarm clock forgets to ring. You wake up late. *Hello, world!* Fatigue and tension greet you with a dull, throbbing headache. But you ignore that. You rush out without even eating breakfast and get to school a split second before the bell rings. With a sigh of relief you sit down in class, ready to pat yourself on the back, when you suddenly realize you left the assignment at home.

The deadline! All that work for nothing! And on top of that, your mean teacher shouts, "Not again! For not turning your assignment in on time, I'm giving you an hour's detention after school. *Be there or else!*"

You sit quietly, depressed, and experience your first migraine headache. And you agonize over this one dreadful fact: *It's only first period!*

You have put yourself in a No-Win Situation. You feel like a loser because you let the situation get out of control. Your teacher sees the bind you have put yourself in and becomes aloof and difficult when you need sympathy and understanding.

This is a situation all too familiar to many students. Without a take-charge attitude and a plan of attack, you too will continue to invite anxiety and emotional stress. And those needless negative feelings spill over into your social life. You spend the whole day snapping and yelling at your friends with little or no provocation.

Finally, your friends turn away from you. *You* turn away from you, and a vicious hate circle takes over—all because you just wanted to get by in school with a minimum of effort and discomfort.

RULE 3. FIGHT FRUSTRATION BY STAYING IN CONTROL AND PLANNING AHEAD.

TAKE CHARGE OF EVERY SCHOOL SITUATION BY LOOKING FOR BETTER ALTERNATIVES.

Teachers are always setting *deadlines* for tests, class work, and other school activities. This makes some students feel tense, frustrated, pressured and uneasy. In short, teachers may make you feel as though you are being thrown emotionally off balance every day you go to school.

FEELING OUT OF TOUCH

SAYS WILMA:

I'm pretty good at getting people to feel sorry for me. I fake a lot of illnesses. Even jumped off the roof of our house once so I would break something. Broke my arm! It hurt but it was worth it in the long run. Everybody kept asking me how I was. It was really great.

Tension

When you worry about meeting deadlines, taking tests, following directions, or worrying about what the teacher is going to get you for this time, you are feeling some degree of tension. You are experiencing tense muscles and nervous strain, and you are going to be easily annoyed with what anyone says to you.

Tension is an unpleasant feeling, one that many students experience almost daily. And feeling excessively tense in school is not healthy for you. Learn to control tension by resolving those situations that make you tense or else you will always be unhappy and uncomfortable in any class-room, with any teacher.

Frustration

Whenever a teacher stops you from doing what *you* want to do, that's called *frustration*! For example, if you're not called on to answer a question, or not allowed to sharpen your pencil or leave the room, that's when you get frustrat-ed and, like a loser, feel defeated.

Homeostasis is a word that means the way people try to maintain their sense of well-being. When we are hungry, we eat. When we are sleepy, we go to bed. And when we need companionship, we naturally turn and talk to those around us.

Some students need to talk to someone who is sympa-thetic. But sometimes, when we have problems and want to confide in someone in class, we invite even more dis-content. It's bad timing when you want to talk while the teacher is talking. Why? Because the teacher quite natural-ly interprets your chattering as rudeness. And that makes for more problems added to those you already have.

What kind of a day are you having right now? Is it riddled with tension and frustration, anxiety and unhap-piness? Is it a typical day? The kind Theresa describes? She is a lot like you, friendly, impulsive, and very talkative.

SAYS THERESA:

> Well, I got up, got dressed, couldn't find my coat again, and dreaded going downstairs to breakfast. My mom gets on my case every morning about coming home late. She's been on me all week about it. But I don't listen to her.

So then I drag myself off to school without my school stuff. I always forget my books. So, of course, the teacher in first period picks on me for being irresponsible. She yells at me for a while. I don't listen to her. Never do.

Second period is not so great either. I was supposed to give a speech in front of the class about "My Most Embarrassing Moment." Wow! I could just die! Can you imagine? I was so tense, nearly in tears from last period. So I just refused to give my speech. I just didn't care anymore. I was feeling so miserable. Nothing was going right.

Well, I was sent to the principal's office and he yelled at me for the longest time. But I didn't listen much. Then he called my mom to come pick me up because I was being suspended. She was so mad.

My day is ruined and it's not going to get much better. Things seem to just keep going down hill!

Are your school days like Theresa's? Is your sense of well-being threatened all day long with tension, detention, and suspension?

School can be a battleground where you and your homeostasis take quite a beating! And the fact that other students feel the same way isn't really much consolation either. There must be a better way to get an education.

The longer you go to school, the more people make demands. There's no doubt about it; you have to grow up, take on responsibility for your own actions, and learn what teachers want you to learn. The question is: Can you meet their challenges and still come out a winner? Of course you can, by using the suggestions and strategies in this book. Remember—learning what others want you to learn can be both incomprehensible and frustrating.

Like a cold or the flu, tension and frustration can easily be passed from one person to another. Even the most irritable teacher can be a victim. And these mixed emotions don't get better all by themselves. They eventually become more intense. So don't sit idly by and watch your problems grow worse. Remember, the biggest school problem you now have could have been more easily resolved when it was small.

Accept the responsibilities of growing up, accept the challenge, and take charge by reestablishing those important working relationships with difficult people in your life.

Hostility

Hostility is a way of showing bitterness, ill-will, and un-friendliness. Teachers are very difficult to deal with when you show your resentment. Losing control of your emotions, yelling obscenities, or throwing temper tantrums are the result of pent-up feelings. But this immature behavior is an ineffective way of solving problems. It simply makes matters worse.

Improve your communication skills; listen and compromise; react in a neutral, more objective way. Resist the temptation to argue, blame, accuse, and antagonize people.

Don't let those No-Win Situations turn you into a loser. That's exactly what you become when you respond with snide remarks, obscene gestures, and an intimidating stance. If you become hostile you wind up feeling worse than you need to feel.

Be alert! Watch out for others who react with hostility in a crisis. Their negative feelings, obnoxious behavior, and antisocial reactions can easily draw you into an argument or a fight. Your friends can unconsciously drag you right into the middle of their troubles if you are not on guard. Hostility between people can be so powerful, that it can block out everyone's sense of right and wrong, distorting good intentions into bad, and that's when the problems grow worse. That's when they become difficult, if not impossible, to handle.

Signs of hostility include:

- Poor language control: arguing, insulting, swearing, making rude gestures.
- Loss of self-control: immature, unresponsive, undependable, forgetful behavior.
- Excessive behavior: hitting, shouting, belligerence, lethargy, tardiness, chronic fidgeting.
- Devious behavior: lying, taking belongings of other students just for fun, destroying personal and school property.

In situations where hostility and anger predominate, no one is ever in control. They are too angry to find better alternatives rationally.

Rule 4. BE CALM IN A CRISIS. BRING CONFLICTS UNDER CONTROL BY DISPELLING NEGATIVE FEELINGS WITH A FRIENDLY SMILE AND BY COMMUNICATING YOUR CONCERNS OBJECTIVELY.

SAYS ARCHIE:

I just can't settle down in school. I'm so uncomfortable. It's really easy to sit for two or three hours in a theater watching a movie. But in school I just can't sit still.

Discomfort

How uncomfortable do you feel in school? Most students experience a certain degree of boredom, nervousness, and physical uneasiness. When you are in class, you may get tired of paying attention to the teachers and may become distracted by outside noises. Students also get upset when the weather is cloudy. It affects the mood and disposition of almost everyone.

Do you get butterflies in your stomach while waiting to be called on to read out loud or to give a speech in front of the class? It is easy to be embarrassed, especially when you are misunderstood or when your voice cracks, changing pitch and intensity right in the middle of a sentence.

These emotional feelings of discomfort may be accompanied by physical ones—hunger pangs, headaches, drowsiness, colds, allergies, and a multitude of other disabilities that make you wish you were someplace other than school.

If you let difficult teachers get on your nerves and daily school situations get out of hand, you are bound to experience an excessive amount of discomfort. That is not good because, without conscious intervention, it can lead to a chronic state of anxiety and misery. That in turn can lead to a nervous breakdown or worse.

Feeling uncomfortable is more than just a handicap to learning. Your body is sending you signals that some serious malaise needs your immediate attention.

There is little cause for alarm, however, if your discomfort is a result of anticipating a major test, giving a speech, or some other learning activity that may cause temporary stress. This discomfort will disappear by itself unless it is compounded by teachers who are continually putting pressure on you. But even here, the discomfort is temporary. It is still only a small problem and can be handled easily. Most students adapt to troublesome school situations with a minimal amount of goose bumps and apprehension.

Here are some effective strategies you can use to decrease the discomfort you might experience in school:

- Make a list of situations that you feel would make you uncomfortable. By writing them down, you can begin to decrease your fear of those situations.
- Share your feelings, fears, and anxieties with those you trust: parents, counselors, other teachers, ministers.
- Get in touch with professionals, persons who are experts on emotional disturbances and discomforts.

Most people you meet, excluding difficult teachers, are more than willing to listen to your problems. Most of them can give you good advice too. They can often see your dilemma more clearly than you can because they are not emotionally involved. So don't despair; there is always a comforting thought in time of trouble.

SAYS GRACE:

Moving is a real downer. I don't know anybody at school. I'm real lonely and homesick. And new teachers you don't even know, yell at you all the time.

Depression

Moving from one place to another, losing friends, the death of a family member, or other misfortunes may get you down. Having the blues, feeling dejected and depressed, is one of the loneliest, most miserable feelings you can experience. If you don't deal with depression, however, you are liable to go into a tailspin, becoming sullen and obsessively moody. This may lead to feelings of anger or even guilt. In the end, you may not want to talk to anybody. And isolating yourself like this from others and wallowing in self-pity is no way to solve your problems.

What you must do is come to grips with whatever is making you depressed. Otherwise, there is a good chance you'll become emotionally and physically ill. Without a strong take-charge attitude, your problems may grow so big that only a doctor can help you.

So take charge; deal with your problems while they are still small. As a first step in recovering from depression, many experts in human relations suggest that you work to develop self-esteem. How? By making the following a part of your daily routine:

- Keep to a daily pattern of doing things.
- Exercise, but don't overexert yourself.
- Do something to help someone else every day.
- Practice relaxation techniques.
- Talk about your problems with people you trust.
- Refuse to shut out the world and the people who are close to you.

Practice these strategies daily and you will be able to guard against devastating emotional upheavals in your life. They can not only help you overcome feelings of depression but also can help you reestablish needed friendships with others.

SAYS TOM:

> I guess I'm dumb since I just can't do anything right. I'm afraid to open my mouth. I'm not the greatest speaker in the world. I don't think anyone really cares if I live or die.

Rejection and Withdrawal

A turtle withdraws from the world by pulling its head into its shell, an ostrich by sticking its head in the sand, and a student by not reaching out, by being unresponsive and afraid of meeting the world on its own terms.

Like depression, the "I-don't-care" attitude is a sign of rejection and withdrawal. Feelings of being slighted or shunned can be very unsettling. Like other mixed emotions, you cannot embrace them for long without serious health consequences.

These feelings make you want to blame others for your mistakes. You feel like giving up in school and settling for poor grades. But doing all of this while rejecting your friends, parents, and teachers will just make you feel worse.

The loser's way is to play the part of the "tough guy" or the "loner," which is a lot like burying your head in the sand. It's a way of building barriers to communication, barriers that shut out the world around you. It's the loser's way because it's the easy way out, but it's a very poor strategy for coping with school, teachers, and personal problems. Why? Because this way spirals downward into a confusing world of self-doubt, ending in a bottomless pit of self-pity and self-rejection.

All right, you say that being rejected by teachers and friends at school hurts your feelings. No argument there! But rejection is no great catastrophe. You can still be a winner! There are always alternatives. Take charge of your life. Look for new and more satisfying relationships. And admit to yourself, "I am not going to be accepted by everyone I meet. And I will not accept everyone I talk to either. But I will try harder to get along with people, no matter what!"

You can take charge of your emotions and at the same time set into motion the feelings of others.

If you think you are a quiet, shy person, you may have a little more soul-searching to do. If you are the kind of person who has difficulty making friends you may need to find the inner strength to cope more successfully with the world. Dig down deep inside of you, find that inner strength, and repeat everyday to yourself, "No matter what anyone says or does to me, *I am still a worthwhile person!*

Always feel good about yourself; be your own best friend. You will be one person you can always depend on, and you will wind up in more Win-Win Situations.

Right now, take charge of your life; enhance your self-esteem by practicing these ten ways to feel better:

1. Develop a sense of humor.
2. Find something to smile about every day.
3. Become interested in school.
4. Be sincere and honest with others.
5. Express your feelings and consider those of others.
6. Be helpful by volunteering when you are needed.
7. Speak in a friendly, pleasant tone of voice.

8. Develop mutual respect in your relationships.
9. Praise generously; criticize sparingly.
10. Lay aside resentment and be more forgiving.

When you feel good about yourself, difficult people are often hard to find. And when you do find them, they are less difficult to deal with. A very wise man, Johann von Goethe, said it this way: "Treat people as if they were what they ought to be and you help them to become what they are capable of being."

This is the way to set into motion positive feelings in those difficult teachers with whom you must deal on a daily basis. They too, are capable of being friendlier and more helpful than you might imagine.

RULE 5. WHENEVER YOU COPE WITH MIXED EMOTIONS, FIRST COUNT UP ALL THE GOOD THINGS THAT HAPPEN TO YOU AND CONTEMPLATE THE NATURE OF CHANGE.

CHAPTER ◦ 4

Handling School
Conflicts

SAYS SALLY:

> School really turns me off. When I do something
> good, you think anyone says anything? But the minute
> I make a fool of myself, everyone's on my back.

School conflicts, especially those brought on by difficult
teachers, are often hard to handle. But even though your
days are full of stress and you feel like running away from it
all, don't. You can make up all the "What's-the-use"
excuses you want. You can turn yourself into a difficult
person, blaming teachers for everything that goes wrong
in your life, or blaming your friends and family for creating
the problems you must deal with. You can feel sorry for
yourself, sulk, and tell everyone, "Nobody understands
me," but don't. School conflicts handled this way will come
back to haunt you. You must decide to take charge and do
something positive to resolve them.

CONFLICTS OF INTEREST

At home you want to stay out until after midnight with your friends, but your parents say you are not old enough and demand that you be home by 10:00 P.M. *OR ELSE!* At school your teachers tell you to be quiet, sit in your seat, and do your class assignments. When you refuse to obey these orders you enter into a conflict of interest situation.

Classroom conflicts are, for the most part, easily resolved. Some, however, linger on for weeks, months, and even throughout the school year. Still others are never satisfactorily resolved.

Interpersonal problems only seem to have simple solutions. It's easy to say to yourself, "If that teacher would see it my way for once, everything would be all right." And the teacher, of course, is saying the same thing. Most school conflicts take a little time to unravel and resolve. They are more quickly disposed of when both teacher and student compromise and look for Win-Win Situations.

Unfortunately, many of these complex problems grow out of personality conflicts and are indeed complicated to unravel. Take Justin, for example. On the surface his school problems may seem petty and superficial. But then again...

Justin, a sophomore in high school, always misbehaves. His parents admit, "Ever since he was born, he has had a short temper. He is always trying to get his own way. It's just his nature."

Justin prides himself on being a "tough guy." He rarely has positive, constructive interactions with his teachers, or with any other adult for that matter. He seems to thrive on intense emotional confrontations.

When asked why he behaves the way he does, Justin shrugs his shoulders. "I don't know. Guess to get the teachers' attention. They don't pay much attention to me when I do what they want."

Positive feedback lets students know that teachers are aware of their presence. If teachers would give praise and recognition whenever possible, it would certainly reduce class arguments and bickering.

But remember, it takes two to create and resolve a conflict. You too are responsible for the bitterness and bad feelings between you and your teachers. You too need to check your behavior. That will help to reduce the stress and tension.

STRESS REDUCERS

1. If you want others to side with you, be on their side.
2. Ask yourself: How do I want to feel? Happy? Contented? Relaxed?
3. Decide how you truly want to live—with or without school conflict.
4. Look for ways that will make you feel good about yourself and others.
5. To feel positive toward others, recognize your own strengths.
6. Begin every day by replacing one *negative* thought with one *positive* thought.
7. Let others be right sometimes.
8. Be open to learning, and to the views of others.
9. Develop a willingness to accept responsibility.
10. Never give up.

With these strategies you can keep your school conflicts manageable. If you don't deal with conflicts effectively, they have a snowball effect. They tend to get harder and harder to handle as the school day goes on, and difficult teachers become more difficult.

Have you ever had a day like this one?

You didn't get enough sleep, so you feel irritable and cranky when you wake up. You have a chip on your shoulder when you get to school, daring anyone to knock it off, to say just one wrong word to you.

Just your luck, your first-period teacher is also starting the day in a mean mood. She glares at you as she hands you yesterday's spelling test with a big red *F* in the center.

Impulsively, you yell, "I don't deserve this. I really studied hard for this test."

The teacher loses whatever composure she has and snaps back, "I don't have to stand here and listen to your insolence."

In such a No-Win Situation, one accusation leads to another, and the teacher finally demands silence and obedience. You counter instead with defiance and rage. The conflict quickly escalates to a shouting match. The teacher does not get what she wants, and you get into a little more trouble than you bargained for. You are sent to the principal's office, where you are chastised and suspended. Your parents are called in to talk with the principal about your misbehavior. In the end, you have made everyone about as miserable as you felt when you first woke up.

NO-WIN SITUATIONS

In a No-Win Situation, there are only losers—plus a lot of anger, resentment, and mixed emotions.

Difficult teachers may ignite many school conflicts, but

certain kinds of students have a way of fanning the flames and being thrown off balance by the very problems they help to create. Such students are caught off guard by having more than their share of family problems, life crises, and personal difficulties. They seem to be out of tune with school life.

Peter is such a case. He has a long history of difficulties with teachers. He likes to disrupt classes by making rude remarks or funny noises or by tapping a pencil on the desk, which irritates his teachers.

Peter doesn't get much sleep. He eats an excess amount of junk food and gets no exercise when he is not in school. In short, he has not taken charge of his own life very well.

He misbehaves in class because he feels stressful about tests, assignments, and other class activities. He becomes very tense toward the end of each period when time is running out and he is only halfway through his classwork. In fact, Peter is usually five minutes behind in everything he does during the day.

His teachers have little patience with his disruptions and abusive language. Peter thinks his teachers overreact when he does something wrong. But that's all right: He gets the attention he craves and accepts the trouble he gets into with little concern.

Here we can see both sides of a No-Win Situation. Peter appears to be marching to a different drummer. He annoys those around him and has no self-control. His teachers are provoked and lose control of the situation, thus contributing to the No-Win Situation.

Perhaps if teachers would listen more to students and threaten them less, there would be fewer classroom conflicts. A little demonstration of moral support and understanding can go a long way.

You don't need to wind up a loser in No-Win Situations. But to avoid them, you do need to take charge of your own life-style. It is very important for you to do the following:

- Get adequate sleep and rest.
- Get plenty of exercise.
- Eat a well-balanced, moderate, and healthy diet.
- Know your own physical, mental, and emotional potential.
- Pace yourself by knowing how fast or slow you work.
- Know your own limits.
- Allow yourself the luxury of being imperfect.

Look for better ways to build lasting relationships. Discuss any bad habits you may have with people you trust. Then take charge and change them. Your parents and close friends may be able to give you advice worth considering.

Always try to resolve your differences with difficult teachers after you have resolved the differences with yourself. Only then will you feel better about who you are and about those with whom you associate.

WIN-LOSE SITUATIONS

In these situations, teachers usually wind up the winners and students, the losers. Take Bob's situation, for example. He is a nonreader sitting in his eighth-grade English class.

Bob loves hot-rod magazines and picture books, but he really can't read past the third-grade level. Whenever his teacher asks him to read a simple paragraph aloud, he slumps down in his seat and refuses. His teacher interprets this as an act of defiance. And thus the conflict begins. The teacher's authority has been challenged on the one hand, and Bob refuses to lose face in front of his friends on the other.

Bob reached the eighth grade while learning a trick or two along the way. When asked to read anything in class, his standard ploy is, "I don't feel well. I'm really sick! I have to go to the nurse's office."

The teacher has tried to give Bob an opportunity to practice reading, so she does not seem to be a loser. Bob gets out of showing his ignorance in class, so he too may claim some minor victory. But the fact remains, when a teacher gives you a failing grade you are definitely the loser. So take care! Those who are in control are the winners; those who are being controlled are the losers.

WIN-WIN SITUATIONS

You automatically become a winner when you stop running away from your problems. So play it smart! Add these three personal goals to your winning strategy: (1) don't expect to be a winner one hundred percent of the time; (2) think and act like a winner most of the time; and (3) instead of shying away from difficult people, take charge, meet them face-to-face, and look for ways both of you can come out winners rather than losers.

The prominent American diplomat and writer Eleanor Roosevelt wrote,

You gain strength and courage and confidence by every experience in which you really stop to look fear in the face...You must do the thing which you think you cannot do.

But you must first find self-respect, and second, mutual respect, for those are the bonds that help keep a relationship strong.

Take a few minutes to be alone every day. Close your eyes and visualize yourself as a winner.

- In any conflict, project an expectancy of confidence, acceptance, and goodwill.
- Mentally plan for success by thinking of each step you must take to face difficult teachers.
- Be a problem-solver, not a name-caller.
- Whenever you anticipate a No-Win Situation developing, compromise.

Adapt to Difficulties

The way you think has a great deal to do with the way you face difficulties. *Think self-control!* Try to feel as relaxed around teachers as you do around your friends, family, and neighbors.

Adaptation means changing your behavior to fit the situation. Be flexible, and be willing to compromise. See the other person's point of view. In that way you won't let setbacks set you too far back, and you won't let difficult teachers make your day too difficult.

But you can't be relaxed when you feel nothing but anxiety—or can you? Most students feel anxious in school from time to time. Anxiety is a normal feeling that can even make us uncomfortable enough to do something about our problems.

We all feel worried or troubled when we face personal

problems. The trick is to put those problems in perspective so that they become less of a problem. So learn to use your anxiety, and then learn to be calm and relaxed, and above all, stay in control. If you do all of this, you will have learned a very important lesson about coping in school and coping with difficult teachers.

Finally, don't forget the old saying, "It isn't what happens to you that matters. It's how you react to it."

A Take-charge Attitude

Some students go out of their way to antagonize and invite the wrath of their teachers by displaying inconsiderate, immature behavior. They create needless conflicts without really thinking about using self-control.

A take-charge attitude does not mean yelling and being defensive. It does mean having a positive, friendly attitude, one that remains calm and in control when it is necessary to resolve classroom conflicts.

The next time you find yourself in this kind of predicament, be responsible; take charge in a more mature way. Don't let your emotions get out of hand. Don't let good friendships and good working relationships go sour because you got "too hyper." Stay in control and always stay tuned in to the beat of school life. Remember, students as well as teachers may be out of sync and difficult, but they are seldom impossible.

RULE 6. BE WILLING TO GIVE AS MUCH AS YOU TAKE FROM ANY RELATIONSHIP AND YOU WILL BE BETTER ABLE TO COPE WITH DIFFICULT PEOPLE.

SAYS GINGER:

I'm me and that's all there is to it. There is no one else like me, anywhere. No one else sees or feels exactly the way I do. And that's OK since I have begun to discover just who I really am. And that makes all the difference in the world.

PLAY IT SMART

There are many ways to stay in tune at school. Knowing what to expect and what is expected of you is a very important part of getting along with others. Check to see which way is the most effective for you.

Information and opinion seeker

This student asks for information, facts, opinions, and ideas because of a natural curiosity. This is a person who attempts to clarify the issues, values, and feelings of others and who is an expert in sensing the moods and attitudes of friends, teachers, and other important people in daily encounters.

Recorder/adapter

Anticipating difficulties and solving problems by identifying the source of the conflicts is what this student does best. He sets his own goals and defines his own limits realistically. He records his ideas in a journal or a diary and maintains a clear perspective of his daily progress. In this way he works toward a more thorough understanding of himself and a more conscious awareness of his relationships with others.

Tension reliever

This student has a pleasing personality and friendly sense of humor. She knows how to help others relax when they are tense and under pressure. She has a positive attitude about herself and others; she demonstrates her sincerity and willingness to help by using her refined communication skills.

Communication helper

This student shows a command of language. He listens carefully to the concerns of others and responds with understanding. He guards against jumping to conclusions, and he is repulsed by those who spread rumors or gossip. He avoids vulgar expressions and very seldom insults, teases, or embarrasses his friends.

Trust-builder

You will not find this student playing malicious pranks on her friends. Her integrity does not allow her to give false information, even in jest. She takes pride in her ability to keep promises, to be dependable, well-informed, and always truthful. She is considerate and caring. She offers moral support to those who need it. In conflict situations she encourages everyone to solve their differences by compromising. She keeps communication channels open by influencing others with her positivism.

RULE 7. PLAY IT SMART! HANDLE SCHOOL CONFLICTS BEFORE THEY HANDLE YOU.

CHAPTER 5

Students Like You

SAYS JENNY:

> If I could change anything it would be school rules so that you can eat food, smoke, chew gum, party, talk all you want, listen to the radio, and have fun with your friends.

Have you ever had a strict teacher, one who enforced every single school policy and class rule? One who wanted to tell you what you should say and how you should act? No wonder you felt as if you had lost control over your own life.

Too often, students try to reassert their will by rebelling against their teacher's authority. They break rules in protest, resisting any controls the teacher may impose. And that, of course, leads to arguments, personality conflicts, and eventually to No-Win Situations. Working relationships break down because a vicious circle of negative feelings and mixed emotions is generated.

Many students become disgusted and give up in frustration. And so grows the saying, "*I hate school!*" They are the losers who do not know how to adjust or cope with school situations. For them, education is not really free— not free from anxiety, irritation, mixed emotions, conflicts, or difficult teachers.

Teachers share the blame for student unrest. The feelings of their students all too often are misplaced under a pile of administrative paperwork, ungraded tests and assignments, discussion notes and lesson plans, and time-consuming attendance records. Unfortunately, sometimes the students' needs and concerns are not very high on the list of classroom priorities.

What are your needs and concerns? To figure out a way to get through the day without getting in trouble? To stay on speaking terms with teachers and friends? To avoid being embarrassed in front of them?

SAYS MIKE:

Do you really want to know what makes me mad? All right, I'll tell you. It's being in your dumb class.

KNOW THYSELF

There never has been and never will be anyone exactly like you. You have always been a unique, one-of-a-kind person. Actually, you are more than that. You are at least three people all rolled up into one distinctive *you*.

First, you are the person others see. They have come to expect certain things of you. They expect you to talk and act "in character."

Second, you are the person you want to become. That is, you like to imitate others. You emulate your favorite sport figures, rock stars, or other people whom you admire or idolize. This innate ability to imitate is not unusual. In fact, the thing most people do best is imitate. We pattern our own behavior after people who have physical beauty, who have special talents, or who meet the rigorous challenges of a particular sport. We may also identify with someone whose cause or philosophy we respect and uphold.

Finally, way down deep is the essence of who you really are, a person who is ever changing, maturing, learning, coping, and adjusting to whatever tragedies and joys life confronts you with. Not everyone sees this part of you because it is so elusive, so well hidden. Indeed, at times this real *you* even eludes you, complicating matters even more. At such times you may feel timid, out of place, or upset without really knowing why. Sometimes you may do something only because it *feels* like the right thing to do at the time.

Thus, when we look in a mirror we see only one person, but not necessarily the person others see nor even the person we think we see. We simply cannot know all there is to know about who we are. That, however, should not deter us from trying, for discovering our potential and our limits is one of life's greatest challenges.

Don't get disgusted and give up in frustration. Find your limits and take charge. Get out of the vicious circle of feeling negative about teachers. Instead, meet them halfway, but with integrity and self-respect.

Socrates, a famous philosopher, put it more succinctly. "Know thyself, accept thyself, control thyself, and above all, be thyself."

Working with People

A working relationship is one in which two or more persons accept one another's point of view, understand their needs and feelings, and share the responsibility of resolving differences between them.

Everyone has a need to be independent, a need to be respected, and a need to feel special. And people need to know what they are expected to say and do. We all need to know our own limits as well as the limits others set for us. Too many rules, of course, are cumbersome and undesirable. But without rules of the road, laws of the land, and codes of conduct, we would feel even more alienated, left out, and confused.

Life becomes more complicated because you are going through a transition period. You are leaving one set of rules that worked well in childhood and are now expected to obey adult rules, some of which you may like and others that you may not see any reason for. Physically, emotionally, and intellectually you are maturing, and the way you accept or reject these rules will determine what kind of relationships you will have with others.

CLASSY STUDENTS

SAYS ALICE:

> If no one can tell me who I am, how am I ever going to find out?

Many studies have attempted to examine and explain the motivations of junior and senior high school students, and you probably know that a favorite pastime of teachers is to categorize and pigeonhole their "good" and "bad" students. Whether you listen to teachers or read these studies, you will doubtless discover that they all paint an incomplete portrait of exactly who you are. Still, the following common attributes are revealing and interesting.

Most secondary students:

- Have a natural curiosity about the opposite sex.
- Think that good manners and other social skills are very important.
- Agree that cheating and stealing are wrong.
- Often have difficulty talking to others about their problems.
- Believe that each person learns best at that person's own pace rather than that of the teacher.
- Think earning good grades is important to their future.
- Are unselfish, sensitive to criticism, and often moody.

Yet, as was just said, each student is unique. You each have a different personality, set of priorities, goals, and problems, and must cope with school difficulties with the social skills that you have learned. Each of you has your own way of expressing yourself, sometimes successfully and articulately, but more often than not in a somewhat awkward and direct fashion. Remember, you are molding your own behavior. You are developing unique mannerisms, good and bad habits, and speech patterns that will follow you throughout your life.

SAYS ANN:

Teachers just don't how to make the lessons interesting. When they teach us math they use these really boring examples to get us to understand addition. Why not give us examples we can identify with? Why not say there were sixteen guys at this party? Then eight more guys came in. How many guys were there now? Now that would really be fun.

As mentioned before, students and teachers seldom see school or each other in the same way. To students, teachers are too lenient, strict, mean, or pushy; with luck, some are viewed as helpful and caring. Most difficult teachers, as we shall soon see, are perceived as unfair, unfeeling, and unfriendly.

On the other hand, teachers are likely to label their students honor students, underachievers, and incorrigibles.

But exactly how do teachers *classify* students? Well, year after year they find the same traits, behaviors, and attitudes over and over again in their classrooms. They see how students cope with school problems, stress, disappointment, and failure.

The next few pages will be even more specific in order to give you a better idea of how students are viewed by their teachers. Basically, they are categorized by commonly observed behavioral characteristics or treated as members of a particular group, and they respond to whatever mental image or set of expectations their teacher projects. Some labels teachers use are the *ideal student*, the *problem student*, and the *impossible student*. Perhaps you will find yourself in one of these classifications.

The Ideal Student

Teachers, from elementary through the secondary grades, all have slightly different notions of an *ideal student*. Perhaps they haven't seen many of them! But to be included in this classification you would be expected to (1) obey class rules and follow directions to the letter; (2) take notes and ask pertinent questions; (3) turn in all classwork and homework assignments, neatly and on time; (4) sit quietly in your seat; (5) look interested in what the teacher is teaching; and (6) avoid engaging in classroom disturbances.

Why, that's impossible, you say? Perhaps. But teachers do have students who are genuinely interested in whatever is being taught, who cooperate and participate with enthusiasm in class discussions.

One important student quality that cannot be overemphasized is *self-control*. Teachers seem to have a more positive rapport and greater willingness to help students who are calm, use good judgment, and handle problems in a rational, mature manner.

The ideal student not only establishes satisfying friendships, and maintains a working relationship with his teachers but also earns higher-than-average grades and has a special charismatic influence that affects everyone he meets.

Juliann is like that. She is a quiet, likable eighth grader from a stable home environment with concerned parents who actively support the PTA and other school programs. Juliann is a straight-A student and has many friends.

She observes limits placed upon her at home and at school. She is able to cope effectively with stress and to find the silver lining in her clouds. When she was elected one of next year's cheerleaders, she reacted with modest pleasure. She delights in competing in track and field events as well as other sports. But how about unhappy events in her life? She has learned to cope with those situations successfully too.

There was a time during Christmas vacation when

she became very depressed. That winter her grandmother, of whom she was very fond, died. And on that New Year's Eve her cocker spaniel puppy ran into the street and was killed by a truck. The Old Year was certainly going out on a sour note. Fortunately, Juliann's family and friends gave her the moral support she needed to get over her depression. She was determined to weather the storm of emotional pain and distress. She was not going to be a loser but rather a winner, with hope and optimism and a positive attitude. She had to work hard to make her future a brighter one, and she did just that!

Juliann learned to cope with her problems in and out of school. She was able to maintain self-control and achieve the goals she set for herself.

The *teacher's pet*, also known as the *apple polisher*, may be viewed by some teachers as an ideal student, although this student is generally less popular in the eyes of friends and even teachers may be repelled by the constant demands for attention.

More than anything else, this student needs a sense of security and importance, needs to feel accepted and to please the teacher and gain praise. This relationship may involve a great deal of mutual respect and trust. The teacher tends to depend on the student to take messages to the office, collect assignments, and pass out books and worksheets.

Other students see the teacher's pet as a first-class phony. Why? Because they are the ones who are reprimanded and criticized. They, not the teacher's pet, must work all the harder to get good grades in class. Thus, the teacher's pet sacrifices peer status for the preferential treatment of the teacher.

SAYS RUBY:

> School's really not that bad. All you have to do is know
> how to get on the teacher's good side. Ask if you can
> help out after class. They really love it when you do
> that.

Another student that can be included in this classification is the *model student*. This student has learned to communicate effectively, maintain self-control, and at the same
time take charge when needed to help resolve classroom
conflicts. Other students turn to her for advice because of
her sympathetic nature and her leadership qualities. She is
sensitive to the feelings of others as she deals successfully
with teachers and peers alike. When faced with difficult
teachers, the model student is able to stand firm and retain
her composure. That is a powerful strategy when it comes
to getting along with people in any situation. The model
student has learned to cope with social and educational
matters without hostile feelings or abusive language.
Instead, this student takes every opportunity to enhance
friendships with a show of goodwill.

SAYS DAVID:

> I feel really good when I can help a buddy out of a
> jam. When you help others, you're really helping
> yourself too. Know what I mean?

Just because you don't see yourself as either a teacher's
pet or a model student doesn't mean that you are not well-
adjusted. And it doesn't mean that you are the kind of
student teachers have singled out as the *rotten egg*. Contrary to popular belief, teachers are not always lurking

around doorways hoping to catch you breaking school rules. In fact, it's not so much how teachers view you, as how you view yourself that really counts.

The *conformist* is another student that would fit into this category. His behavior, however, may go to extremes.

If you are a *conformist* you avoid arguments at all costs. You tend to agree one hundred percent with whatever anyone says. You observe all school rules and follow all directions without question.

But if anyone chastises you for making a mistake, you fall apart. For example, when a teacher rebukes you for giving a wrong answer or for chewing gum in class, you take it as a personal affront and feel that you are being unjustly accused and you sulk for the rest of the day.

Here are five personality traits that teachers observe in the conformist:

- Has a fetish for neatness.
- Has an exceptionally legible handwriting.
- Is generally considered a perfectionist.
- Turns assignments in on time and asks for extra credit if the work is finished before the others.
- Acts in a mature manner.

SAYS SHARON:

Did I follow your directions? Is my writing OK? Is there anything else I can do? No? Well, how about letting me correct some papers? I can take that message right down to the office for you. No trouble.

So far, these are the major characteristics that teachers generally cite in their ideal students. They are the ones who are eager to comply with teachers' demands and expectations. They make it a point to maintain a good relationship by being interested in what is being taught, working diligently, and causing as little trouble as possible.

SAYS BRAD:

> Kids tease me. It's OK. though. I just tell on them when they break class rules. I sharpen the teacher's pencils, pass out stuff, and sometimes do her bulletin boards. I think she really likes me!

SAYS VERA:

> I hate school because you have to work, and I hate work. I also hate waking up in the morning, because I like to sleep. I also hate getting in trouble, because I hate staying after school when I want to go home.

The Problem Student

Studies show that while teachers agree less on the predominant behavioral traits of *problem students*, there are some general agreements. These students (1) don't listen well, nor do they follow directions; (2) wander around the room more than others, making innumerable trips to the wastebasket or pencil sharpener and hand-delivering notes to others; (3) turn in messy, incomplete assignments; (4) chatter constantly; (5) challenge the teacher's authority with rude gestures and language; and (6) appear impulsive and insecure and project feelings of inferiority.

A problem student has difficulty adjusting to school and to teacher expectations. She is likely to come from an environment where family problems are more pressing than homework. Parental unemployment, child abuse, and a variety of other problems—including pyschological ones such as lack of self-esteem, motivation, and personal goals, antisocial nature, and nonconformist attitude—are among the overwhelming, problems he must face. No wonder problem students:

- Are excessively truant.
- Have little regard for the welfare and safety of those around them.
- Are aggressive, defensive, and uncomfortable in social relationships.
- Have a destructive nature.

Some of these students appear hostile, moody, apathetic and withdrawn, or simply unresponsive. Teachers see these tendencies as signs of laziness, irresponsibility, and ignorance, all behavior traits that they feel obligated to change.

Unfortunately, this is where the seeds of unrest and discontent are sown. Class conflicts begin to grow. Why? Because the teacher does not always have an accurate picture of the students. As was said at the beginning of this chapter, you are a very complex individual, one whom no one fully understands—not even you!

Still, teachers consider it their job to evaluate and classify you, for better or for worse. When their perception of you is one of laziness or ignorance, they set out to change you. And then you perceive those teachers as being very difficult: They want you to be something you are not.

Out of the classroom and under more favorable conditions, you may be someone else. You may be very intelligent and highly motivated. You may respond in a friendlier manner when others show more respect for who you are, more sympathy for what you have to face, and more concern for your future. You may be a totally different person when invited to share in a caring one-to-one relationship.

Without a little sympathy and understanding, many students get caught up in difficult situations. And many students let such situations get the better of them.

Take the case of Terry, for instance. He had been in and out of trouble for most of the school year. He was considered a problem student by his twelfth-grade teachers.

Terry shunned his friends and remained alone and unhappy after he returned from the spring break. He had spent the entire vacation at home, doing nothing. None of his friends called him; none of them came around to play basketball or cruise the main drag at night. He thought he would be glad to get back to school to see them, but he wasn't.

Back in school, he felt listless and bored. He refused to go to dances, sports events, or other school activities. He tried to convince himself that he really wasn't depressed, but he felt keyed up and very nervous. For the most part, he felt "blah" about everything.

His parents argued all the time; they had no time to help him with his homework, or with anything else. for that matter.

Terry quickly lost interest in school. He did not turn in assignments and failed most of his tests. He was unable to keep his mind on his studies. His teachers saw the change in his behavior but could not understand it. Nothing seemed to interest him. He went through the motions of going to school, sitting in class, and getting by, but didn't put forth much effort.

One day, near the end of the spring semester,

Terry's mother, who was now beginning divorce proceedings, was asked to meet with the principal. By now everyone had become concerned about Terry's poor grades and his defensive attitude. The principal wanted Terry to be evaluated and placed in the school's counseling program, but his mother refused to give permission. Saying, "I just can't deal with your problems right now. I've got problems of my own," she stormed out of the office in a huff.

So Terry is labeled a problem student because teachers who are responsible for the education of many students don't always understand all the circumstances surrounding each individual.

Indifferent students, like Terry, refuse to listen or follow directions. Instead, they become inattentive. They have lost the incentive to achieve their own goals or even to work with others.

Teachers seem to be more and more difficult as this student persists in negative classroom behavior. They are frustrated watching a student who has a great deal of potential become apathetic and show callous insensitivity toward those who want to help. If the teacher is willing to help, that's all right; if not, that's all right too. If the teacher is patient and helps the indifferent student with an assignment, the student will not resist or complain. On the other hand, if the teacher is irate and difficult or decides to kick the student out of class, so what? No big deal!

In short, the indifferent student has developed a defeatist attitude, becoming convinced that anything that is done to meet others halfway will only be futile.

This student sees school as a waste of time but attends anyway to get away from a home environment filled with tension, hate, and even physical abuse; or because some authority figure has said, "Hey, it's the law! You have to go to school, *or else!*"

Furthermore, the indifferent student may not find school to be very challenging. On the other hand, he may not have developed his thinking, reading, writing, or math skills to the fullest. And he knows it, and he know *he can't win!* If he tries, he proves to everyone that he is a failure, or so he supposes. So grows the saying, *I hate school!* But he still comes.

The indifferent student has not developed the necessary communication skills to get along with others. He responds to friendly gestures with wisecracks, counters with disdain or vulgar remarks, or is simply unresponsive and apathetic. He is nonetheless easily identified by teachers, who anticipate his reply to almost any question, "I don't know," even when he does know.

If it were not for his negative demeanor, which is usually written all over his frowning face, he might be mistaken for the *silent student.*

The *silent student* is a problem because she is not at ease, especially in the classroom. Extremely timid and self-conscious, she hates to be called on. She speaks so softly that even those right next to her have a hard time hearing what she says.

The teacher is forever admonishing her to "Speak up! Talk louder! Say what you mean!" It is almost impossible to carry on a dialogue because she draws back from the spotlight; to her the attention focused on her is a frightening ordeal.

The silent student's communication ability has not been fully developed. She feels that anything she has to say will be insignificant or trivial. Thus, she feels inferior when participating orally.

That, of course, makes the learning process even more

difficult. The task of teachers is to help students express their ideas in a cogent, intelligent manner. They do so by encouraging students to read orally, give speeches, act in plays, and participate in many other group activities.

The silent students, few though they may be, come into conflict with those difficult teachers who insist on putting them in the spotlight. Both students and teachers find themselves at odds, in awkward situations filled with apprehension, negativism, and self-doubt. Neither seems able to take control of the interaction necessary to create a Win-Win Situation or a comfortable working relationship.

Interestingly, when the silent students are outside the classroom, they may be as friendly, as talkative, and as uninhibited as their peers. They may feel more comfortable under circumstances that are more informal and less demanding.

The *class clown* is constantly in conflict with his teachers. He thrives on the attention gained when he burps, makes obscene noises, shouts, and in general disrupts the class with his antics. He doesn't mind being rejected or laughed at by his peers, nor does he seem concerned about being reprimanded by his teachers. He is often at the bottom of the class "pecking order," being teased and tormented by everyone. But whether negative or positive, the attention given him is what he desires most.

The angrier he can make his teachers, the more delighted he is with his tomfoolery. The more chaotic the class becomes, the less control the teacher has and the more freedom his classmates have as they join in, increasing the noise level. Eventually, both students and teacher wind up in a No-Win Situation. The teacher, unable to cope, becomes frustrated and severely reprimands the class clown along with others. Thus, instead of learning, students find themselves fighting a difficult teacher who "just can't take a joke!"

Class clown is a role being played by more and more students who are less than serious about getting an education. The class clown is even admired for breaking rules and the monotony of an otherwise boring school day. But he also doesn't seem to have much control over his own behavior. Feeling no accountability for the pandemonium he creates, he revels in his irresponsible shenanigans. Consequently, he is the ones who is sent to the principal's office, who is given detention, who is tongue-lashed for his misconduct.

Yet the more he gets in trouble, and the more difficult his teachers are, the better he likes it. His infamous reputation becomes a badge that he wears proudly, showing everyone that he is a force to be reckoned with!

RULE 8. FIND THE COURAGE TO MEET LIFE ON ITS OWN TERMS. BE RESPONSIBLE AND MATURE NO MATTER WHAT SITUATION YOU FIND YOURSELF IN.

Another student that irritates teachers is the *sneaky student* who in subtle ways tries to disrupt the class. He waits for the teacher to turn her back to the class and then begins to shoot spitballs, throw paper airplanes, or slyly pass the new girl's purse across the room. He hides other students' books and personal belongings in the trash can. Seasoned teachers look there first when chalk, erasers, or the roll book turn up missing.

The sneaky student is a master of trickery and deception. He is the con artist of the class. He is seldom caught because he has learned how to blend into the class with an innocent glance and gesture that says, "Who, me? You must be kidding. I didn't do anything wrong!"

Like the class clown, he is only interested in breaking the monotony of classwork as he blows a hidden bird whistle in his mouth or squirts other students under the desk with his camouflaged squirt gun. But he never draws attention to himself. He waits until the teacher is busy taking attendance, writing an assignment on the blackboard, or helping another student before going into action.

Fortunately, there are not too many of these students either. Most teachers try to ignore the disturbances, realizing that their childish behavior is intermittent, and not too serious. In fact, the teacher's relationship with this student may even be friendly and easygoing; however, it is definitely not built on mutual respect and trust.

Of course, there are many other kinds of problem students whom teachers might consider "minor leaguers." For example, the *five-minute student*, who always asks, "What are we supposed to be doing?" right after the directions have been explained twice. And there is the *oops! student*, who has an expression of bewilderment on her face as she walks around saying, "Oops! I forgot my books! Oops! I forgot my homework!"

Finally, every once in awhile you run into the *no soap student*, the one who has flies buzzing around his head and a rancid odor about him. He wears his smelly gym clothes month after month without thinking to take them home to be laundered.

These students have failed to take control of their lives, to be responsible for their own actions, and to maintain any kind of working relationship with others.

These problem students, who have no strategies to work through problems successfully, turn out to be losers. For them, school has become nothing but a hassle, a place where difficult teachers become even more difficult. They wind up feeling insecure about themselves. They struggle through school, year after year, but it is a struggle!

At the secondary level, some students go through school with very few friends, with no real incentive to graduate, and no one to turn to for moral support. These students often find school overwhelming. So they lose the will to keep trying and give up all hope of being successful. At that point, they become what teachers refer to as the *impossible student*.

RULE 9. YOUR PROBLEMS ARE ALREADY HALF SOLVED ONCE YOU FULLY UNDERSTAND THEM.

The Impossible Student

If you are an *impossible student*, you probably have a very low opinion of yourself. Making friends is difficult if not impossible. Others sense your lack of empathy or caring for anyone, including yourself. They tend to ignore those who are unfriendly and noncommittal, who aren't dependable and don't keep their promises.

Most teachers characterize the impossible student as one who (1) has very poor communication skills; (2) is restless and extremely uncooperative in class and may have serious learning disabilities; (3) demonstrates extreme mood swings; (4) labels teachers as difficult, "the enemy," mean, or too demanding; and (5) learns remarkably better in a one-to-one relationship.

The impossible students seem to be living in the fast lane, defying everyone's authority, feeding on adversity, playing verbal games that are insulting and embarrassing to peers and teachers alike.

Their offensive language, behavior, and attire serve only to alienate them from others in school. They invite those around them to scorn and hate them, apparently feeling more comfortable with rejection than with companionship. However, they are always asking teachers; "Why are you always picking on me?" and "Why don't you leave me alone?"

At one time or another, most students exhibit some type of extreme behavior, if only to show that they are one of the gang. This simplifies the teacher's job of classifying the impossible student. Lesson plans are readily altered or simplified, lines of conduct more clearly defined, and teachers wind up in the winner's circle when student misbehavior turns into a Win-Lose Situation. In short, the deck is stacked in favor of teachers.

So, of course, their natural tendency is to respond negatively to students who appear selfish, self-centered, or emotionally out of control. Only a very few of these impossible students hover on the border line of juvenile delinquency, but unfortunately they leave their mark in school.

News item: A high school student was expelled from the district yesterday for possession of a controlled substance. The 15-year-old flipped out after being caught smoking marijuana in a rest room.

News item: Students took over a seaside resort during spring break, hurling rocks and bottles at police officers who attempted to disperse the unruly youths.

News item: Firefighters battled a school blaze for two hours late last night. Two students were arrested at the scene. One student admitted, "I just wanted to get even with my shop teacher for giving me a bad time and lousy grades." He later added, "It all started when my father beat me black-and-blue for bringing home a report card full of *Fs*."

News item: Rival gang members were arrested on the grounds of a junior high school yesterday after a fight broke out. Saturday night specials, knives, and lead pipes were confiscated. Razor blades were found in the pocketbooks of female members, who were also searched for weapons. Thirteen students were taken to County Hospital for treatment of minor cuts and injuries.

These news items represent extreme cases involving impossible students who are more appropriately classified as juvenile delinquents. Because they are under the jurisdiction of law enforcement agencies, this book will only discuss those students who are less violent but are still a constant source of school disruption.

If you are a *nonconformist*, you are seen by teachers and friends as one who sets himself apart from others. The nonconformist is unconventional, refuses to obey school rules and class directions, and is very argumentative, taking sides with the underdog or any unpopular issue.

He has little regard for others or their belongings. In fact, he steals for the sake of stealing. He also writes on school desks and walls and sets fire to trash cans just for fun. Others, of course, see his vandalism as an antisocial action. He is usually shunned by other students.

If you think you are a member of this group, see how familiar the following comments sound: "This is really stupid! You can't make me do that! I don't have to do what you say!" If you are still in doubt, take the following quiz to see if you are truly a candidate for this classification.

Nonconformist Quiz

1. Do I like to do things my own way *all* the time?
2. Do others think I act strangely?
3. Am I too sensitive?
4. Do people stare at me or give me funny looks?
5. Do I have difficulty communicating my feelings to others?
6. Do I overreact when teachers criticize me?
7. Am I always suspicious of other people's motives?
8. Do I argue too much?
9. Am I the only one who really knows what's going on?
10. Do I have only one friend?

If you answered yes to more than half of the questions, chances are good that you belong to the *Club for Nonconformists*.

Teachers find the nonconformist an impossible student because he is overly critical of his peers, antagonizes and berates his teachers, finds fault with everyone but himself, and is often sent to the principal's office for being belligerent, uncooperative, or for committing any number of infractions.

The *prima donna* is another student who has trouble interacting with teachers. She is self-centered and thinks school rules are meant for everyone else. The prima donna is usually found strolling into class a few minutes late each day, chatting with friends on the way to her seat, ignoring the impatient stance and stare of the teacher. Reprimands for misbehavior seem irritating but mostly just dumb.

The prima donna doesn't take school very seriously anyway. When the teacher assigns her after-school detention, she conveniently forgets and is seen laughing and joking with friends.

If you are this kind of a student, you enjoy hours of endless gossip. You feel that your social life is much more important than anything that could possibly be taught in school.

Teachers are constantly scolding these students for not paying attention. Mirrors, compacts, and combs are preferable to them than pencil, paper, and textbooks. They too find most teachers very difficult.

The *recognition seeker* schemes and plans ways to get the maximum amount of attention from his friends. He stays up nights thinking of practical jokes he can play on them.

If you are this kind of student, you may think you're a real party animal, a wild and crazy person. Your mind is not on school. Getting good grades and passing tests are just not important. What is important is having fun at the expense of others, especially those difficult teachers. At the same time you ask yourself: "What am I doing here? Hey, how come I'm not skiing, boating, at the beach, or doing a million other things instead of sitting in this boring class?"

The recognition seeker does like being in school, even if he won't admit it. Why? Because boring as school may seem, he enjoys being the life of the party in his classes. Getting himself and others in trouble is a small price to pay for having such a good time.

Teachers usually find these students impossible to handle because there are at least two or three in every class. Each one, of course, is competing with the teacher and the other students for class attention. Teachers wind up reprimanding them for horsing around and for being disruptive. Eventually, they are given detention or sent to the principal's office. No matter. To them life is too short to get serious about anything.

The *dropout* is by far the most impossible student. She is unable to establish any kind of relationship with teachers or peers. She is unable to keep up academically or socially with those her own age. Naturally, she feels out of place and misunderstood. But that may not be the real reason she doesn't go to school.

She may have a language problem that prevents her from learning at a normal pace. She may not be motivated to learn. She may be disenchanted with school and with life in general. She may come from a broken home, living with only one parent or a guardian who doesn't care whether she goes to school or not. The dropout may feel she has to stay out of school to support a family by working at odd jobs or by other less reputable means.

In addition, she may have some serious emotional problems of her own. The dropout may also have severe psychological problems or have physical or mental handicaps that preclude her attending classes.

It is not within the scope of this book to analyze the many complex factors that contribute to an ever-increasing rate of school dropouts. But they are overwhelming and for many students impossible to cope with. That is why approximately three thousand students quit high school every day; nearly a million students each year leave school before they complete twelve years of education. Sadly, about a third of them never even reach the ninth grade.

If you are thinking about dropping out of school, get the facts first. Write a letter to

The National Dropout Prevention Center
Department P
P.O. Box 248
Clemson, SC 29634

Ask them for all the facts before you make this major decision. The center gathers the latest information for people who are considering leaving school early. Its network of experts can help you make the right decision.

Take charge of your life. Cope with difficulties by first coping with yourself. Find intelligent advice and alternatives. Develop the power to adapt to difficult situations by adjusting your behavior and attitude.

TEN WAYS TO COPE WITH YOURSELF

1. Find *self-respect* first, and mutual respect second.
2. Maintain *self-control* in all situations.
3. Accept *full responsibility* for your own actions and learn to achieve your personal goals.
4. Be *confident* and *calm* during personal crises.
5. Develop a sense of *humor*.
6. *Understand others* as they are, not as you want them to be.
7. Take each day in stride. Find time to *relax*.
8. *Keep asking questions*.
9. *Don't drop out*! Instead, get the knowledge that will make you happy, productive, and successful throughout your life.
10. For yourself alone, today, acquire the gift of a *positive outlook* for your own future.

CHAPTER 6

Types of Teachers

SAYS MARCIE:

Teachers are just plain mean. They're always yelling
when we get on their nerves. Would it hurt them to
be nice for a change?

Students have definite ideas about good teachers and
bad ones. They advise their friends which classes to take
and which teachers to stay away from, based solely on their
own experience with a particular teacher. "This teacher is
easy. She hardly gave us any homework. But watch out for
that teacher. He'll drive you crazy with his weekly book
reports."

What are teachers really like? Is their only goal in life to
be as difficult as possible?

Well, one of the main concerns of a teacher is to care for
the safety and welfare, academically and socially, of the
students. Not everyone will agree that this is a primary
function of a teacher. In fact, not everyone will agree on
exactly what teachers should say or do, what qualifications
they should possess, or what personality traits are most

desirable. Teachers, like their students, are all unique and all have their own strengths and weaknesses.

Parents expect teachers to teach one thing, students want to learn something else, and teachers bring a special knowledge all their own into the classroom to share with those who want to listen and learn.

There is wide diversity of opinion as to just what teachers should teach and how they should teach. School boards, administrators, college professors, students, and educational writers are all fascinated with the study of teaching styles and methodologies.

A vast amount of research also reveals some interesting viewpoints from student populations. They describe good and bad qualities of teachers, descriptions that are usually subjective and always subject to change. So, at best, research and student opinion polls paint only a vague picture of teachers. Still, some thought-provoking generalizations can be made as this book examines why teachers behave the way they do.

As was already seen, teachers are constantly classifying their students. But students also size up their teachers. From a student's viewpoint a teacher may be a *popular teacher*, a *"Who cares" teacher*, or an *impossible teacher*.

These classifications will be studied not to stereotype, but to examine familiar teacher characteristics so that you can gain an understanding of how to cope successfully with teachers who behave in certain ways.

The Popular Teacher

Every student looks for something special in a teacher. Generally, all would agree that their favorite teacher must (1) be fair but friendly, willing to help with personal as well as academic problems; (2) be enthusiastic rather than dull and boring; (3) be intelligent and have a positive attitude about teaching; (4) have a sense of humor; and (5) create a learning environment free of chaos and distractions.

Mutual respect and self-confidence are also necessary teacher attributes. Students feel that these qualities enhance teaching and at the same time decrease the incidence of situations laced with tension and frustration.

Mr. Ferguson, an energetic ninth-grade social studies teacher, is popular because students sense his sincere desire to help them fit into his classes comfortably.

An out-of-state student, Frank, transferred to the small Midwestern school district in the middle of the fall semester. Having been told by other students to watch out for Mr. Ferguson, Frank naturally was nervous.

Mr. Ferguson sensed Frank's trepidation and realized his need to establish relationships with his classmates, so he took a little extra time to dispel any myths of meanness that surrounded their working relationship.

During a field trip to a historical museum, Mr. Ferguson tried subtly to help Frank make new friends. The trip was a success and so were his efforts. Friendships developed, cultural gaps were bridged, and Frank returned to the classroom enriched by both academic and social experiences.

Like Mr. Ferguson, a *model teacher* is enthusiastic and always willing to interact with students in a positive, caring manner. This teacher plans class activities around the needs of the students, setting class goals so that each student will not only feel challenged but also have a sense of satisfaction when those goals are achieved.

She enjoys sharing ideas and stimulating students' thinking, but she is also an exemplary listener, expressing her acceptance of student feelings and thoughts with genuine concern.

Furthermore, she has the patience to answer the same question over and over again until everyone understands. For this reason, unfortunately, the brighter students in her class who catch on quickly may consider her boring and repetitious.

The model teacher is dedicated to her profession, expends a great deal of energy, and finds herself mentally and physically exhausted at the end of the day. Contrary to popular belief, she is not superhuman. She doesn't provide action-packed, nonstop lessons and activities seven hours a day, five days a week for approximately one hundred eighty school days a year. But she is a very effective teacher, and her students respect her for her no-nonsense approach.

The model teacher, then, has a deep understanding of human relationships, and she patterns her own communicative behavior to circumvent student-teacher conflicts. She comforts the frustrated student and smooths ruffled feathers. She provides many Win-Win Situations by her guidance and leadership abilities. Finally, she is able to laugh at herself and her own mistakes while never ridiculing or embarrassing students in her class.

You may have a little trouble with the *brilliant teacher*. He is amiable and very knowledgeable about his subject, and he has many years of teaching experience. He is also very dedicated, however, and seems to feel that he must be right one hundred percent of the time. He answers each and every question, usually in more detail than you care to hear. Basically, he is candid and unpretentious in his relations with students, but above all he is devoted to his subject.

The brilliant teacher is popular because students admire his intelligence and understanding of his subject. However, he can be tedious, and for that reason students tend to have difficulty communicating with him. He likes to talk more than he likes to listen. He is a bit egotistical and feels that what he has to say is the most important.

In an Information Age such as ours, there is a real need for teachers who keep pace with new knowledge and social change. Unfortunately, a good researcher is not always a good teacher. The brilliant teacher usually has an excellent grasp of theories and abstract ideas that it is not possible (or appropriate) to pass along to his neophyte students. This may be frustrating to his attempt to design realistic classroom goals. Thus his teaching style is not as dynamic or as effective as that of the model teacher. In fact, he uses too many technical terms and foreign phrases, making note-taking difficult and class discussions boring.

This teacher may even have poor speaking habits and use of gestures. His lectures may be monotonous and uninspiring. He knows what he wants to say but at times lacks a well-organized way of saying it.

The *creative teacher* is popular because she is imaginative, robust, talented, and resourceful. She is able to open the minds of her students by bringing new meanings to old ideas. She has the unique ability to perceive relations between objects, thoughts, and concepts, connecting the seemingly unconnected.

Her teaching style includes the use of audiovisual equipment, slide presentations, tape recordings, photographs, artifacts, and other teaching materials. She has excellent communicative abilities and encourages her students to improve theirs through group discussions and debates. She is always devising lessons that will increase student interest and participation. Students like her because she is artistic, inventive, and perceptive. She enjoys talking about what they like to talk about—the World Series, national and local disasters, terrorism, political candidates, and current events.

She is a teacher with whom you can easily establish a working relationship. She is friendly and confident. But most of all, she is willing to listen. She encourages you to experiment and make mistakes as long as you learn from them. At the same time, she will discourage others from embarrassing you or dwelling on your shortcomings.

The creative teacher maintains a rather informal, easy-going relationship with both teachers and students, but, like most popular teachers, she lets you know her limits. She, too, is a no-nonsense educator. Because of her teaching style, shy students are apt to feel more secure and less inhibited in participating in class. Yet those who are more outgoing sense when they have reached her limits.

Look alive and be alert when the *gung-ho teacher* enters your classroom. He is a very energetic, dynamic, "go-getter" teacher and is usually the one who demonstates the most school spirit. His team-oriented teaching style is ever present in class. He rewards straight-A students with gushing praise. Contrariwise, he is appalled by the "slackers" or those who resist being team players.

Still, he is not vindictive. With his positive, gung-ho attitude, he has a very forgiving nature. That's why students place him in the popular teacher category. His concern for them is honest and sincere, evidenced by his constant praise. It is well to pay close attention when he explains assignments and gives directions though. His teaching style demands that you do exactly what he says when he says it. Like any good drill sergeant, he will tolerate only a minimal amount of inattentiveness.

He tends to assign an excessive amount of homework, often forgetting that you have other demands on your time such as part-time jobs, home chores, and extracurricular activities. Like other teachers, he does have his bad days, snapping orders and barking at students for minor infractions. Yet you sense that his bark is worse than his bite, that deep inside he remains a resilient, caring person.

So far we have focused on the popular teachers, those who are basically likable, who are able to establish rapport and maintain a good working relationship with students. A few teachers, however, are not as easy to be around. They are the ones who have lost their enthusiasm and energy; they are often said to be "burned out." They are the "Who cares" teachers.

The "Who cares" Teacher

Some teachers leave a lasting impression. Others you take for granted day in and day out. In fact, you can hardly remember what they look like on the second day of summer vacation. They are the "Who cares" teachers.

This type of teacher has her own unique set of idiosyncrasies, odd speech habits, and mannerisms. She may be very temperamental, or she may be insensitive and hurt your feelings unknowingly. Or she may take great pleasure in nagging and needling you. But, all in all, she never gives you much cause for alarm or puts you under any real stress.

Students characterize the "Who cares" teacher as one who (1) is moderately intelligent but also a bit insensitive and lethargic; (2) has no sense of humor; (3) is usually not too friendly and at times can be very mean; (4) lacks enthusiasm and originality; and (5) often seems defensive, insecure, and intimidating.

This teacher is unable to keep her students interested in her subject. Because of that, chaos and unruliness reign in her classroom. Students concentrate on doing what has to be done with as little effort as possible. These teachers are in teaching, but teaching is not in them anymore.

The purpose of education is not to have students sit in class hour after hour and argue with their teachers over rules or be reprimanded for minor misbehavior. Nor are they there to be given busywork and boring assignments. Instead, there should be a caring relationship between students and teachers, one that encourages students to grow into intelligent, responsible citizens.

The burned-out teacher provides very little concern or education. He is forever taking attendance, writing hall passes, sending messages to the office, and taking care of a multitude of clerical jobs in the classroom. He never discusses assignments at any length. He seems to have too little time for teaching because he is either passing out worksheets or collecting last week's assignments.

He is quite content as long as you are working quietly at your seat. This gives him time to write on the blackboard, rearrange the drawers in his desk, or enter grades in the roll book.

The reason this teacher feels burned out is that he teaches the same thing year after year. He feels like a TV rerun. He copes with the same excuses and problems from one predictable semester to the next. He sees himself going in circles, getting nowhere as a professional educator.

His students sense this attitude, and they too get caught up a "Who cares" restlessness. Class is boring, little teaching is taking place, and learning is neither enjoyable nor rewarding.

Some teachers are just the opposite. The longer they teach, the more they ramble on without saying much. These teachers are aimless talkers, according to their students. This teacher is dedicated and cares about her students. She thinks she is the font of all knowledge because of her many years of worldly experience. She enjoys lacing her lessons with anecdotes and pointless stories. Over the years, her tall tales have become a major part of her teaching style.

This teacher's singsong voice gives away her "Who cares" attitude. She has gone through the same classroom discussions so often that she has regards her style as being comfortable; but to others, her communication habits and her way of doing things seem automatic and stale.

SAYS IKE:

You better pay attention to your teachers. You'll fail for sure if you think all teachers are boring. Sure, they talk too much, but you can learn a lot from some of them. That's no lie.

Teachers are supposed to set an example. They are supposed to teach you to remember things. They are supposed to help you remember to turn in homework on time, to bring your textbooks and school supplies to class. They are supposed to help you learn logical procedures. But have you ever had a teacher who was always forgetting things? Did one of your teachers ever lose track of what she was saying during a class discussion? Did one of your teachers ever forget to return your test, or worse, lose it?

A few teachers have desks cluttered with books, ungraded papers, bulletins, and a collage of other school paraphernalia. These desks may reflect the teachers' cluttered thinking.

The Absentminded Teacher

This teacher has too many other things on her mind, things more important than where she misplaced her grade book, room key, or briefcase. She seems very intelligent, perhaps too intelligent. She has a bland personality and no sense of humor, and students rarely see her smile. When accused of being forgetful, she reacts with indignation.

You may have some difficulty maintaining a working relationship with the absentminded teacher, but with a little extra effort you can cushion the effect. First, remember to write your full name and ID number on each assignment you turn in. Second, try to place your work in the middle of the collected pile of assignments; that way it is less likely to be misplaced. Third, never turn in work too late; always turn it in on time. Finally, be especially alert when graded work is distributed. If you don't get yours back, bring it to her attention immediately, even if you don't think it will do any good. And ask her to check her grade book to see if she gave you credit for the lost assignment.

If all else fails, try one of these alternatives: Ask if you can redo the assignment and turn it in later. Begin keeping duplicate copies of all work in that class by using carbon paper, a copying machine, or even a computer and a printer.

Students complain when teachers seem uninterested, when they don't listen to all sides of an argument, or when they make up their mind ahead of time about an issue. Many students consider these *narrow-minded teachers* difficult because they are either unfeeling or overbearing and for the most part reveal a definite "Who cares" attitude.

This teacher is biased and opinionated. He generally does not tolerate debate on a topic under discussion. Students groan in despair when they hear him say, "Don't be stupid! Why, when I was your age. . . ."

This teacher sees every issue in absolute terms; that is, either all right or all wrong, all black or all white, no gray areas or middle ground. His attitude is clear when his last words on any matter are, "I don't care to listen to that silly nonsense! *I know* you are just too young to understand or appreciate the facts anyway!"

This is a teacher who is set in his ways. For that reason alone, you are likely to run into real trouble, especially if you get too emotional, feeling that you have to prove your point. Don't argue with him. No matter how deeply you feel about what you believe, arguments will be exercises in futility. The time and energy you invest will yield only frustration and conflict. You will never be able to get your point across because he is a person who sees and believes only what he wants to see and believe! You must keep your emotions in check if you are to get along with the narrow-minded teacher. Listen carefully, and then take what you hear with a grain of salt.

* * *

Finally, there is the *ho-hum teacher*. Her favorite expressions are, "I know! I have heard it all before. Nothing surprises me anymore!" She is a veteran teacher who has had perhaps too many years of teaching the same thing over and over again, who has come to believe that nobody cares about getting an education anymore. Certainly, no one seems to care about doing her assignments or turning in her homework. Why? Because she conducts the class and answers questions in a halfhearted way, with little enthusiasm or rapport with her students.

She lacks classroom control. Her disciplinary practices are too lax or ineffective. Thus, paper airplanes, spitballs, and other objects are continually sailing across her room. Familiar four-letter words are scribbled in classroom dictionaries and textbooks by her rowdy students. And the noise level is, by and large, earsplitting!

Fortunately, the ho-hum teacher is becoming extinct. With support and funding throughout the country in the 1980s, education reform, quality teacher-training programs, and no-nonsense teaching practices have become top priorities.

Still, you may be scheduled into a class or two with teachers who have lost interest in teaching, who wish they were working at another job. In these classes you have every right to yawn, complain, and label school *boring*. You may even want to request a transfer into another class. But before you do, be sure that the teacher is at fault, not you. If you are frustrated and having difficulty getting along with your teacher, evaluate your situation first by asking yourself these questions:

- Is the teacher really boring or am I the one who is just bored with school in general?

- Do I try to get involved in the learning situation by asking questions?
- Do I volunteer during discussions or participate willingly in class assignments?
- Do I disrupt the class more than others?
- Who is really to blame for my low grades and lack of interest?

When you have answered these questions honestly, talk to your parents, the school adviser, and the principal to see what other arrangements can be made to help you cope with this difficult teacher.

SAYS DOROTHY:

Teachers just care about getting paid, not about us kids. They should care more, and not be so boring. I have my problems too. And I need teachers to understand me better. We aren't their kids, so they don't care. Anyway, you can't teach teachers how to care. My math teacher cares. He has kids of his own so he knows what it's like.

STEPS FOR COPING WITH "WHO CARES" TEACHERS

Step One

Be alert to the idiosyncrasies of your teachers. To maintain a close working relationship with them, practice being agreeable, attentive, and tactful. Also, be sensitive to their moods by observing such nonverbal clues as facial expressions, posture, and tone of voice.

Step Two

Be sympathetic even when a teacher is stretching a point. Instead of becoming argumentative, be neutral. By being a neutral, sympathetic listener, you not only avoid saying things that you might regret later, but you also stop yourself from jumping to conclusions that may get you into trouble needlessly.

Step Three

Be objective and maintain a positive, take-charge attitude. If you become too defensive, you will fall victim to those old familiar No-Win Situations. What you don't say can be just as important as what you do say. Teachers, too, may have some underlying motive that may not make sense to you until you hear their side of the story.

Step Four

Be clear when you express your own ideas. Then stand back and compare them to the teacher's point of view. If you try to force your ideas on others, they will only become angry. Instead of arguing, maintain your self-control. That way, you will be able to resolve differences more effectively.

Step Five

Be more mature. Be willing to admit it when you are wrong. Let the other person be right. This will be a big plus for you and will usually catch the "Who cares" teacher off guard. You create a Win-Win Situation for yourself by giving in a little, or compromising. Most teachers tend to back off emotionally and reconsider their own words and actions at that point.

SAYS TED:

> School is a real bummer. You can't even walk out of the room for a minute without asking your teacher's permission. These rules are really crazy.

The Impossible Teacher

Students are in full agreement here. All teachers can be impossible once in a while; some more often than others. There will always be one or two to whom you just can't relate, no matter what you do.

Why are teachers impossible or extremely difficult? Students know the answers to that question! Teachers (1) just don't understand students; (2) are mean and moody; (3) are self-serving, only thinking of themselves; (4) are either too wishy-washy or exert too much authority in class; (5) are insecure and have poor leadership qualities; and (6) cannot relate to students because they are out of touch, and don't know how to communicate.

At times, teachers themselves admit that they can be irritating, distraught, and too strict, especially at the end of a school day when nothing has gone very smoothly. Teachers can also be insulting, unfeeling, and they can embarrass their students on purpose in front of their friends, hurting them for no apparent reason.

Students know when teachers have lost the desire to teach. They lose the empathy needed, and they forget how to interact. Perhaps that is why teachers are accused of losing their sense of humor, of never smiling, or of never being able to laugh at themselves and their own mistakes.

They are grouchy, complain, and yell more than they should. Perhaps that is why they become overly critical of others, from the school administration right down to students who never come to school. These teachers have turned into cynical, disillusioned, fault-finding persons.

The following are comments and reactions from students who have had to cope with one or more of these *impossible teachers*:

This Teacher:
  Hates us!
  Constantly scolds us for every little thing.
  Doesn't care about our feelings.
  Accuses us of things we don't do.
  Is tense and nervous and too strict all the time.
  Brings your grade down if she doesn't like you.
  Can't control students.
  Never listens to what we have to say.
  Won't give us a chance to explain.
  Acts snooty, like a real know-it-all.
  Is always bossy.
  Thinks students are trying to get the best of her.
  Treats everyone like a little baby.
  Is never friendly, never smiles.
  Doesn't give us any freedom in class.
  Always loses our assignments and her temper.
  Is hard to understand.
  Is sarcastic when we ask questions.
  Wants to know too much about our personal lives.
  Cannot be trusted to keep secrets.

Sound familiar? These reactions are undoubtedly the result of negative feelings, poor communication, unconcern for student feelings, and misunderstandings that are usually at the root of classroom conflicts. Once students begin to realize what their teachers are really like and why they act as they do, frustration, tension, and eventually personality conflicts disappear. When students know what makes a teacher tick and then adjust to the teacher's behavior, there is a real chance for a working relationship to become established.

SAYS PRISCILLA:

> Teachers think they know everything. Well, I don't think they do. They are too self-righteous and strict. They make us feel dumb because they win every argument. And one of my teachers always accuses me of being the class clown. It's just not true, but she calls me this anyway.

Impossible teachers are impossible only until you begin to understand them. For example, one of the most disliked *and* misunderstood teachers is the *authoritarian teacher*. His teaching style is not at all popular with students because it includes being very strict, dictatorial, and assertive. He feels he must never lose control over the class, so he demands obedience and strict adherence to the rules, *all* of the rules! He is a stern, "by the book" teacher who severely punishes anyone who breaks even the most insignificant school rule, such as chewing bubble gum or arriving ten seconds after the bell rings. He just sits there and waits for you to "make his day!"

An authoritarian teacher can be extremely difficult to deal with, especially if he feels that the class has gotten out of control. Like Dr. Jekyll and Mr. Hyde, he may be very happy, sincere, and caring one minute, then turn right around and yell at you without listening to any excuse or explanation. If you overreact, you fall into his No-Win Situation. So don't lose control.

Remain calm. Otherwise tempers will flare, and you will be the loser. Try to maintain whatever positive relationship you may have with him. Why? Because you must come back to his class again the next day, and the next day, and the next! When you stay in control, you stay out of trouble. It is to your advantage to get a passing grade rather than to get kicked out of class.

Another strategy you can use with the authoritarian teacher is to *let him be right!* It's easy, and it works too. Why? Because this strategy lets him stay in control of himself as well as the class.

In fact, this strategy will help you make friends with almost anyone, difficult or otherwise. Just remember, it's OK (for you) not to be right all the time. Hear others out for a few minutes, and let them be right, even if you don't agree with what is being said. Once you do that for people, it's amazing what they will do for you. And the best part of the strategy is that you really don't have to do anything. Just step back and let the teacher be right by staying neutral and in control.

The next time you get caught up in an argument that is not particularly significant anyway, *stop!* Say, "I guess you were right. I hadn't looked at it quite like that before." Then, for a few moments, be neutral and friendly. Those few moments you give others to be right are extremely important moments for both of you.

Watch the teacher's reaction. He will be caught off guard, and there will probably be a long, awkward moment of silence and some reflective thinking on his part. He will realize that you are not challenging his authority.

Thus, you will have effectively disarmed a potentially stressful situation.

Like the authoritarian teacher, the *impulsive teacher* is very headstrong. She can be "sugar and spice and everything nice" one minute, and the next a worker of iniquity, hovering over you, chastising and yelling. This teacher is also quite difficult. She is hot-tempered, explosive, and easily provoked. She overreacts to classroom situations. Becoming flustered, she may shout such pet phrases as, "You better behave or else! I won't put up with your nonsense!" Students cringe in their seats, hoping she isn't pointing at them and squirming as her high-pitched, screeching voice echoes through the room, a sound almost as painful as fingernails on the blackboard.

The impulsive teacher can be hyperactive at times. She seems edgy and nervous. She often loses her train of thought. Thus, she becomes a loser, but so does everyone else in her class. If you find yourself at odds with this teacher, talk to your school adviser and your parents to see if some alternative can be worked out. In the meantime, remember what La Rochefoucauld, a French moralist, wrote: "We all have strength enough to endure the misfortunes of others."

The motto of the *nitpicking teacher* is, A Place for Everything and Everything in Its Place. He is very fussy, very exact. Neatness and accuracy are of utmost importance. He is appalled by students' slovenly habits, rude language, impolite manners, and sloppy work habits.

You have three choices when you cope with such a difficult teacher. You can (1) sit befuddled and confused, feeling sorry for yourself, and simply fail the class; (2) play his game, nitpick right back at everything he says and does, in which case you will still wind up the loser; or (3) deal with him as a challenge rather than as an insurmountable obstacle to your education. Strive for neatness and accuracy in his class. The least that can happen is that your handwriting will improve a bit, and you might even become more conscious of important details and procedures in his particular subject matter.

This teacher is difficult to cope with because misery loves company. Some teachers will go to great lengths to make students, especially those who are obnoxious and uncooperative, feel as miserable as they do. So stay out of his line of fire and act in a mature manner. Also try the following strategy.

First, as with other difficult teachers, be neutral and friendly. Arguing or creating a conflict with this teacher will only turn your good days into bad days. Ask only necessary questions.

Second, keep things in perspective. Be calm and don't get tense. Remember, you have to stay in his class for one period. It is only one of six or seven classes you have. So don't let him spoil your day.

Finally, keep a daily log or diary of what bothers you in school. Put your thoughts in a notebook. Write down what happens between you and your teachers during the day. Record your feelings, negative and positive, about your classes, and you will find that getting through a school day is a lot easier. Keeping a written record of your personal feelings and school frustrations is an effective strategy for dealing with seemingly unmanageable situations. At least, that's what Patty discovered.

Patty was a tenth-grade student at Arlington High School. She could not get along with her history teacher at all. In fact, she disliked him so intensely that she almost had a nervous breakdown. She was letting his negativism overshadow her entire life and became unable to concentrate on her schoolwork or pass her tests.

Fortunately, Patty's favorite teacher, a physical education instructor named Ms. Lang, listened to her problem in confidence and then offered some good advice. Ms. Lang suggested that Patty keep a daily log of everything that went on in her history class. She was to write down as many positive comments as possible. She was to find something to like about the class each day, such as the arrangement of the room, the way students dressed, or the kinds of friends she had. Patty was to be as honest and sincere about her feelings as possible. She knew that she would be the only one who would ever read her daily log.

At first, Patty thought this was a dumb idea, a waste of time and paper. But she was desperate, so she gave it a try. Ms. Lang said that it would decrease Patty's headaches, tension, and overall mental anguish.

Patty was diligent. She wrote every day about how friendly the students were, the warmth of the room, and other positive comments that made her feel better little by little. She even tried to pick out one positive thing a day about the teacher, the way he tossed chalk in the air while talking, his expressions, dress, stance, and other mannerisms. Each day she read and analyzed the previous day's entry just before going into class, and it made her feel a lot better.

She continued to write, read, and analyze her daily log until the end of the semester, when she received her grades. They were still nothing to brag about, but that wasn't what was important. She had learned to change her attitude from negative to positive, and that *was* important! She even told Ms. Lang, "I realize now that part of the teacher's problem was really part of my problem. I guess I was expecting too much from him. And just knowing that I can change my feelings about school and other difficult people is worth a lot." She smiled and walked away. No thanks given, none expected!

Patty's strategy will work for you if you give it a try. You will be able to handle tough situations and get rid of negative feelings that might otherwise stay bottled up inside. It really does help to write about your problems in school and about your feelings toward difficult teachers.

Finally, there is one other teacher who is unable to get along with her students. She exercises authority in excess and really has difficulty communicating. She also may have some personal problems of her own. She is the one who is angry all the time, the *excessively mad teacher*. Your impulse is to give up, throw in the towel, and talk to her as little as possible. Your standard response to any of her questions may well be, "I don't know!" or "No! Nothing's wrong, nothing at all!"

The excessively mad teacher sees only what will fit into her jigsaw-puzzle world. Any piece of information that isn't perfectly obvious or logical infuriates her. She can see no rational explanation or excuse for what you say or do, no way to make your world fit into hers.

She likes to argue with you. Why? To show off her pseudointelligence! To students, she seems to rant and rave about details, and she refuses to give an inch even during unimportant squabbles. Students are generally wary when they sense her abruptness, her bickering ways, and her phobias, especially her "controllaphobia" (that's fear of losing classroom control). She teeters on the verge of paranoia at times.

That's not her only fear either. She fears criticism from

administrators, parents, and colleagues. She worries that everyone is out to get her. As a result, this teacher tends to distance herself from students and others. Yet, deep down inside, she craves acceptance and companionship. When she is calm, she appears to be artificial, not personal or real. When she teaches, students feel that she is hiding her true self and putting on an act. When she is mad, this teacher is a time bomb, exploding into fits of anger during the school day, sometimes without provocation. She is filled with self-doubt, tension, and fear.

You may feel there is no hope when coping with an excessively mad teacher. But wait! Don't give up! Don't ever give up hope! There is always an alternative, always a strategy for you to pull from your bag of tricks. Being antagonistic or insensitive to her feelings will not work. Instead, you should (1) discount her negative effect on you and the class; (2) not hold a grudge and make her your problem; (3) find out what she *is* interested in, what she likes to talk about; and (4) ask yourself: "Does she really need my hate, or my understanding and acceptance?"

This teacher, like all the others we have mentioned, first entered the field of teaching because she felt she had something of value to contribute to the well-being of others.

It may be difficult to act friendly, and you may have to struggle to keep a positive attitude in her presence, but that is part of taking charge, staying in control, and maintaining a working relationship.

Show *goodwill*, not animosity, toward difficult people or anyone for that matter. If you do, you will usually avoid saying things you might regret later.

Abraham Lincoln did not have teachers in mind when he made the following statement. He was talking about a far simpler matter—the Civil War. "There are two ways to destroy your enemies; one is by brute force. By this method, neither of you are hurt; the better way to destroy an enemy is by changing your enemy into a true friend."

SAYS CHUCK:

> I'm telling you, this teacher is really mean. "No" must be his middle name. Does he let me sharpen my pencil? No. Does he let me borrow a piece of paper? No. Boy, does he get to me!

RULE 10. DISARM THE NEGATIVISM OF OTHERS BY SHOWING GOODWILL TOWARD THEM. YOU CAN PRODUCE A POSITIVE EFFECT ON THOSE WHO CARE ABOUT YOU.

Make it your first priority to achieve your personal goals in life. Then make it your second priority to be more successful in school. But remember, to accomplish all this you cannot afford to make enemies or to hate people just because they happen to be teachers, bosses, or adults. Only *dropouts* fall back on this lame excuse when they can't get along with others or when they just can't wake up in the morning to go school, or later on when they fail in life, the most important class of all!

CHAPTER 7

The Teacher's
Behavior

Research shows how important it is for students and teachers to like one another. Students do better in classes, have a more positive attitude, and are more willing to follow directions from teachers they admire and get along with. Mutual respect is the foundation needed in this kind of relationship. You are more likely to work harder and earn higher grades for someone who truly cares about you as a person. However, that does not imply that because you are a poor speller you had a mean or difficult English teacher, or that because you are not good in math or science you had teachers who were not very good.

The point is that teachers have a profound influence on the way we think, how we feel about a subject, and even our personal preferences in life. The way a teacher teaches, his personality, and his behavior affect impressionable minds in a classroom. Ask yourself: "Did I learn to like or dislike certain things because of my home life, or did school and my friends have something to do with it?"

All of your teachers will try to influence your thinking, and will tell you what they think is good or bad, just as your parents do. But what is good, even to adults, does not always make "good sense."

Another problem with defining good behavior arises from an adult's point of view versus a student's viewpoint. Sometimes parents and teachers forget that you see life a little differently, that you are learning for the first time things that adults may take for granted. So doing the right thing at the right time isn't as easy as most people think it should be.

The next time you feel confused or irate about a teacher's behavior, or about your own, recall the words written by a sixteen-year-old girl, in a letter published in the Chicago *Daily News* by Kathi Elliot a few years ago.

Dear Mom,

Today isn't any special day, but I need to let you know before I say it. Mom, I'm mixed up and there are so many decisions to make. Each minute seems so important and I want to make it last forever. Each day escapes so quickly and I can't do everything at once.

I guess you feel pushed out of my life and that I only love you when I remember. I know it isn't right, Mom, but I keep forgetting that life will continue after today. You learn that tomorrow always comes and I can't have everything now, you keep telling me, but I guess I can't believe it even though in my soul I know you're right. Mom, I need to try things out. You experienced it already and know how silly my dream-chasing is, but I need to learn on my own.

Someday I will look back and laugh at myself, but now I must experience life and search for my purpose here.

I'm sixteen and I'm an adult, but sometimes I forget and I'm a child once more. I fall down a lot and my ego is often bruised and I always run to you to make it better, until I remember that I can't turn back. I must stand on my own two feet.

Experiencing what is new to us through trial and error is often mistaken for misbehavior, especially in school where we attempt to behave in ways that may be comfortable for us but perhaps not for those around us. At school there is too much emphasis on getting the right answer rather than on learning from our mistakes. That's part of the reason why conflicts arise between you and your teachers. Furthermore, a teacher's behavior may not conform to *your* expectations. She may even appear to be antagonizing you when she shouts, "Settle down! Behave yourself! Don't act foolish!" And this, of course, is said with good intentions and in the name of education.

Yet most teachers do want you to learn from your mistakes. Bernard Shaw, a famous writer, put it this way. "A life spent in making mistakes is not only more honorable but more useful than a life spent in doing nothing."

So go ahead, make mistakes, but learn from them too! You have that right. Give all teachers a chance to help you through those confusing, trial-and-error experiences. Confide in teachers you trust and in those who are willing to work with you. Learn never to make the same mistake twice, and then pat yourself on the back for learning that very important lesson.

RULE 11. GETTING THE MOST OUT OF EDUCATION AND LIFE IS KNOWING THAT THERE IS A CHALLENGE TO BE MET.

Everyone has a distinctive personality that must be accepted and adjusted to naturally. The same is true of teachers and their teaching style. Most of them are easy to get along with. The impossible teachers, however, have some specific behaviors worth mentioning. Try to think of ways you can adapt to them, take charge, influencing them and creating a Win-Win Situation for yourself.

Being too abrasive. What you would like to say to a teacher who exhibits abrasive behavior is: "Why can't you stop being so mean for once and just be agreeable?" She is a pompous, rude, unfeeling person who thinks she can do no wrong. But, in fact, she accuses her students of being what she is: disagreeable, immature, and conceited. Her aggressive behavior is quite contagious too. Students sense it, and they imitate it. It encourages a vicious circle of never-ending No-Win Situations. And what happens to the learning process in a classroom filled with mixed emotions and mayhem? Well, you, as a student, already know the answer to that!

Why are some teachers so rude and abrasive? For one reason, they create a smoke screen to hide their personal feelings, their nervousness, or inexperience. Some teachers are on a superego trip and don't even know it! New teachers, though, may actually be hiding their feelings of insecurity and doubt behind their cold, stern stares, strict rules, and abrasive, get-tough communication patterns.

What can you do when you come face-to-face with such a teacher? First, understand that effective communication and sparkling personality are not her strong points. That means you will need to use more self-control and patience when coping with her since she is unresponsive, unfriendly, or unconcerned about you.

Second, don't become emotional or upset. Instead, be objective and neutral. Decide whether your own expectations toward her are unrealistic. Is she the one who is abrasive, or are you projecting your own negative feelings into every encounter with her?

Finally, compare notes by asking other students how they feel about her behavior. See if they object to her teaching style as much as you do.

In general, learn to adapt your behavior to whatever style and whatever personality you come up against. Don't fall into the trap of being abrasive or pushy yourself. Let the abrasive teacher feel she is right even if you don't agree with everything she says or does. There may be outside forces you know nothing about that make her act the way she does.

As with any impossible teacher, if all else fails seek advice. Talk with your parents and get their support before you approach the principal or student adviser in an attempt to transfer to another class.

SAYS TOM:

> What makes me really mad is when teachers pick on you when you make mistakes. They get even madder when you talk to your friends when you're supposed to listen to them. They really have some mean tempers. How can you possibly like them?

Being angry. Anger is a very strong emotion, one that can easily erode both friendships and working relationships. Too much of it can threaten your sense of well-being, throwing your balance out of whack. When a teacher becomes angry and yells at you, your first impulse is to strike back. That's the nature of anger, but when we give in to this negative emotion we become losers, and that is exactly what makes school conflicts so complex and difficult to resolve. And so the dilemma: Should we give in to our feelings, or should we accept the challenge, take charge, and think things through to a logical, objective conclusion? It is to be hoped that you said the latter. Should we yell back at teachers who yell at us? Should we take the loser's way out and throw a temper tantrum or storm out of the classroom? Did you say no? Why? Because you will fall into the same old No-Win Situations that have got you in trouble before, those situations that got so out of hand that the teacher simply kicked you out of class and you threw up your arms in disgust shouting, "*I hate school!*"

By now, however, you know better alternatives, more effective strategies when you meet a teacher who is always angry. No one is asking you to fall passionately in love with this teacher, or even to show false admiration. But try to be friendly, stay in control, and communicate responsibly.

Defuse the angry teacher's aggression with a calm and mature reaction. It will show goodwill and a genuine concern to find a Win-Win Situation. This will not be easy to do at first. It will take courage and a little practice. But you will be a winner if you just remember this: Two people can stay angry twice as long as one!

There is always an alternative to anger. For example, you can quickly, quietly, and very calmly size up a teacher and her reasons for being difficult. See if you can help decrease her anger and her desire to yell at you. It is really up to you to take charge, to defuse a conflict. If not you, then who? Don't think for a moment that any person who is angry, yelling, ranting, and raving is in control of anything! That is why it is so important for you to stay calm. Speak to this angry teacher in a softer than normal tone of voice. That by itself may alleviate the teacher's anger.

RULE 12. YOUR CHALLENGE IS NOT TO ELIM-
INATE THE ANGER IN OTHERS;
RATHER IT IS TO CONTROL YOUR
OWN REACTIONS.

Baiting students. When was the last time a teacher poked fun at you in front of the entire class? He may have chided, "Don't take it so seriously. We were just injecting a little harmless humor at your expense." Remember how you felt embarrassed, how you hated him for leading you on, baiting you in front of your friends?

Although teachers scold students for teasing and tormenting others, they can be as guilty as anyone when it comes to taunts and tasteless jokes.

They are also the ones who keep telling you, "Don't say that. That's vulgar and disgusting. Why must you be so insulting?" and, of course, their old standby, "Just do as I say, not as I do!" Remember that one?

"But they aren't being fair," you say. No argument there. You're absolutely right! But the teacher *is* the teacher. There is nothing you can do but let him bait you into No-Win Situations, right? *Wrong!*

Your winning reaction to baiting behavior is a friendly, good-natured one. Don't take ridicule and teasing personally. Being baited and even insulted is all part of school life.

Getting angry or taking these kinds of insults personally makes you the *loser*. Don't let this verbal battle of wits bother you and you will come out the *winner*. And students who like to play this game but cannot make you mad will usually stop bothering you and go tease somebody else. The game begins in a playful spirit but often winds up in a Win-Lose Situation where feelings are hurt and friendships are terminated.

Never play this game with teachers either. You'll lose more often than you'll win. Teachers should know better than to engage in such childish bantering, but they too like to show off their quick wit by embarrassing you in front of the class. After all, the teacher *is* the teacher! So the odds are against you. If you try to insult the teacher in class, even in fun, you run the risk of having your grade lowered, being called a smart-mouth, or worse. Furthermore, your playful attitude may easily be construed as disrespectful and belligerent and you may wind up in the middle of a No-Win Argument.

Your winning reaction, then, to this baiting behavior is friendly and neutral. Smile! Why? Because it is difficult for people to insult or put down others who are friendly and good-natured. If this strategy fails, however, talk over the problem with a close friend or someone you trust, someone who will let you complain, criticize, and blow off steam. By confiding in someone when you are upset, you are able to calm down and get back the self-control you lost.

Being too demanding.   Some teachers want everything done in a certain way—not your way, but their way. If you skip part of a question on an exam, or fail to follow every single direction they give you, these teachers act disgusted. In fact, they may even threaten you with a failing grade.

Now, a few students and teachers believe that a failing grade is of little consequence. They believe that grades are arbitrary and are poor motivators in today's educational system. For example, students who are given the choice between doing their homework or receiving a failing grade for not doing it will usually opt for the latter. Why? Because they just want to get through school day by day with the least amount of effort and discomfort.

Some students, however, hold just the opposite attitude. They try to figure out what kind of grading system each of their teachers uses. In that way, they discover which classes to study for and which ones will be a snap.

You have probably heard some of your friends say, "Let's party! Forget about studying for that test. It's a waste of time. You're just going to flunk it anyway!" On the other hand, you may want to listen to that inner voice of yours saying, "If you do study, your chances are better than if you don't!" Grades, whether anyone wants to admit it or not, do have some influence on the kind of future you will have, the career that you will finally decide on, the college you choose, and the kind of life you will live.

So it is essential to learn to cope with teachers who are demanding. For losers, teachers' grading systems may seem intimidating and unfair, but you, as a winner, think of each teacher's style of teaching and evaluation as a challenge, not an insurmountable obstacle. Most of all, don't let any teacher's demanding behavior turn you into a failure. Don't join those unhappy students who left their education behind, never developing to their full potential, never learning how to cope with failure.

Ironically, many demanding teachers are the ones students remember best after they do leave school. They are the teachers who gave too much homework, too many tests and quizzes, and assigned chapter after chapter of nightly reading. They are the ones you will look back on as the teachers who taught you the most.

Dealing with these demanding teachers, then, is like dealing with other difficult teachers. Have a friendly, positive, take-charge attitude and meet their challenges. Stay in control and on good terms with them and your cooperation and efforts will be rewarded.

> RULE 13. IF PEOPLE SENSE THAT YOU HAVE A HIGH OPINION OF YOURSELF, THEY WILL ALSO SHARE THAT OPINION.

This book has examined a few specific teacher behaviors that annoy students, that may give you cause for concern. We have a better understanding of why some teachers seem more difficult than others, and why we feel the way we do about them. So what more can we do to keep the lines of communication open, to be less tense and frustrated during class? How can we maintain a viable working relationship with all teachers? Easy! Try this:

FIVE-STEP STRATEGY FOR COPING WITH TEACHERS

Step One

The most valuable single step you can take in preparation for coping with teachers is to *stop wishing they were different*.

Step Two

Put some distance between you and those difficult behaviors displayed by teachers. The more you can see others as truly separate from yourself, the more you will be able to see them as they really are.

Step Three

You know how negative some teachers can be. That's part of their nature. But they also have a reserve of positive feelings and reactions that *you can tap into*. If you can avoid doing and saying those things that make them respond to you negatively and focus on ways to improve your interaction so as to encourage positive, friendly, and productive responses, you will be more successful with those teachers. Your relationships will last longer and be stronger, and you will find yourself in more Win-Win Situations and in a friendlier atmosphere.

Step Four

Devise ways to create more Win-Win Situations by *developing a take-charge attitude*. Solve your differences constructively, not destructively.

Step Five

Sharpen your listening power; it is one of most effective communicative powers you have when it comes to coping with personal crises both in and out of school.

CHAPTER 8

The Power of
Communication

Do you remember the last time you were sitting in class wanting to ask the teacher a question but you felt tense, awkward, and uneasy? Does it seem that everything you say gets mixed up, that no one understands you because your words come out all wrong? On top of that, you listen but you can't make head or tail of the teacher's assignments or directions.

Well, many students feel exactly that way, some more than they let on. The fact is that successful communication between teacher and student doesn't happen automatically. You must really try to make yourself understood. You must take charge and take advantage of every opportunity to improve your communication skills, to become a powerful, effective communicator.

Interestingly, you cannot not communicate! Why? Because there are no "stop signs" in communication. You and your teachers are constantly interacting and communicating on both verbal and nonverbal levels.

You may not be expressing your ideas well enough, or your teachers may not accurately interpret what you say even if that is their job. They speak, direct, assign, and reprimand you in an attempt to change your behavior and your attitudes, and your beliefs and ideas on a variety of topics. And what about your communicative efforts? Everyday you speak in your attempt to manipulate and influence your friends as well as your teachers. *That's the nature of getting an education!*

Some days conflicts arise because your communication gets out of control, you lose confidence in yourself, and you get too emotionally involved in school situations. Remember, daily conversations, class discussions, and social communication all have one thing in common: They have a powerful effect on what we think and how we act toward others. When we say things we don't mean or regret later on, we lose control and we know we are losers. We get angry and upset and say things that get us in trouble. In fact, one of the main reasons why we say we hate school is because we get ourselves in trouble *using words and ideas* indiscriminately, inappropriately, or incorrectly—nothing more! But that's enough, because the result is usually a classroom in which students yell and scream and chaos and confusion reign. Thus, when teachers and students are not in control of their communication, their relationship deteriorates, tension mounts, and conflicts are created.

It is all too easy for good communication to turn into bickering and argument.

People do have a tendency to speak before they think, and that's what gets them in trouble. Their ideas are not always well thought out or expressed, and the effect of their words on others is either unpredictable or disconcerting. That is why good communication is not only an asset in school but also an essential skill that you will need to be a winner as you develop satisfying relationships and meet personal challenges throughout life.

The student who has poor communication skills is handicapped. He cannot adapt to school situations or the people he meets there. His behavior is often inappropriate because he has not learned to relate to others. Instead, he is misunderstood, becomes easily discouraged and frustrated, and communicates ineffectively by:

- Insulting others and making them feel unwanted.
- Being a source of embarrassment.
- Pointing out the mistakes and faults of others.
- Acting conceited or superior.
- Using obscene language and rude gestures.
- Being argumentative.
- Seeming narrow-minded, prejudiced, or arrogant.

RULE 14. THINK FIRST, THEN RESPOND TO PEOPLE IN A POSITIVE, FRIENDLY WAY.

If you want to improve your relationships with others, be more self-confident, have a positive outlook on life, and improve your communication habits. But before you can do that you must first like yourself and accept the way you are. That's the foundation for most Win-Win Situations. Plan for your future. Set goals that you want to achieve, and when those goals are achieved you can look back with pride and self-confidence.

A Daily Program for Improving Relationships

The program is based on the ideas of Sibyl F. Partridge, who wanted to help people increase their self-confidence and at the same time decrease their daily frustrations. Begin by saying:

JUST FOR TODAY I will adapt to what is, change what I can, and find peace of mind in the process. I will interact harmoniously with my family, my school, and my friends, setting my worries aside until tomorrow.

JUST FOR TODAY I promise to be happy for a little while, believing what Abraham Lincoln once said: "Most folks are about as happy as they make up their minds to be." I will search inside until I find contentment.

JUST FOR TODAY I will like myself. I will exercise and be strong. I will read and keep my life in focus.

JUST FOR TODAY I will be agreeable. I will dress neatly, talk softly, praise others, and be courteous. I will resist the temptation to argue or make others feel hostile toward me.

JUST FOR TODAY I will do something *for someone* without expecting a reward. Then I will do two other things for myself that will help me become more mature, more responsible.

JUST FOR TODAY I will do something I don't like to do but know is necessary. I will cope with people and situations that are difficult, knowing that they are only difficult, *not impossible.*

JUST FOR TODAY I will face part of my problem but will not try to solve it all at once. I will strengthen my relationship with others, and I will look forward to a better day tomorrow.

JUST FOR TODAY I will write down, hour by hour, all the things I expect to accomplish. I will not follow this exactly, but at least I will try, and by trying, I will eliminate two demons of frustration— *hurry* and *indecision.*

JUST FOR TODAY I will relax for half an hour. I will think of how much better off I am right now than a million other people living in the world today.

JUST FOR TODAY I will not be afraid to smile, to love, or to see what is beautiful and good. I will not be afraid. Instead, *I will be a winner!*

Set your own goals, and make this daily program a part of your life. You have nothing to lose! At the very least you will begin to like yourself and others more. Difficult teachers will be less difficult. You will find mutual trust in your personal relationships, improve your communication efforts, and increase your self-confidence. Can you find a better way to take charge of your life? If not, give this program a try. Go back and read it one more time.

RULE 15. FIND YOUR GOAL IN LIFE, BUT NEVER MAKE UNREALISTIC DEMANDS ON YOURSELF.

COMMUNICATION PROBLEMS IN YOUR CLASSES

Are you afraid to meet teachers head on, eyeball to eyeball? Have you ever asked yourself: "Why me? Why can't I talk to that teacher, anyway?" Perhaps it's because you have not adopted a take-charge attitude, or you lack self-confidence, or you don't think it would do any good. But don't blame yourself for all the misunderstandings that go on in your classes.

Communication can break down suddenly for a variety of reasons. Some factors contributing to communication problems include (1) constant distraction, (2) language/semantics barriers, (3) lack of feedback between teacher and student, (4) status differences, and (5) poorly developed listening and questioning skills. These will be discussed in detail. Some valuable strategies that you can use to offset their negative effects will also be discussed.

Distractions

At the beginning of a class period the teacher gives students an assignment. Normally the students begin their work with a minimal amount of noise. But when they are distracted by people entering and leaving the classroom; office messages blaring over the intercom system; ringing of bells—police, ambulance, and fire engine sirens reverberating in a nearby street—or even just the coughing, sneezing, fidgeting, tapping of pencils, and other noises generated by thirty-five students trying to cope with physical discomfort and mental anguish, communication problems are bound to occur.

All of this commotion and noise can easily trigger an overload response from the brain. We become irritated because we don't like to be distracted, but we also feel powerless to alter the situation. What is the natural tendency of students? To join in, to add to the noise and make the most of it, releasing pent-up tension and frustration. Completing any assignment then becomes a secondary priority. Why? Because students have lost their power of concentration along with their interest and motivation to learn; because students cannot ignore or screen out distractions no matter how hard they try.

It is a well-known fact among educators that teachers must give important directions and information at least three times before the majority of the class finally understands. Students with short attention spans simply give up and begin to daydream or talk with their friends. And the increase in the classroom noise level is inversely proportionate to the patience of the teacher!

It takes a great deal of energy and concentration for you to filter out what is not important and retain the vital information. By simply knowing that distractions work against you, you are more likely to ignore them and to limit their effect. One of the main differences between a model teacher and a difficult teacher is that the model teacher takes the responsibility to ensure a serene, quiet learning environment.

Semantics Problems

Another communication problem that occurs in the classroom is semantics; that is, the relationship between you and words, signs, and symbols. This problem is all too common. Students think they know what the teacher said, but they don't! Why? Because, the teacher may be using words in a new or unique way.

Understanding what is said and what is meant is not always as easy as it seems. It is not uncommon for students to hear something completely different from what the teacher actually said. For example, when was the last time you heard a teacher assign you a list of spelling words to learn, or a set of math problems to solve, and you did the wrong ones?

What about foreign students who do not yet have a command of English? Their communication problems are compounded by such idioms as "dead as a doornail," "sick as a dog," and "fork in the road." Reading between the lines for double meanings is taken for granted by some, but not by all.

Still another semantics problem occurs when a teacher uses jargon or educational terminology. For example, a teacher may refer to instructional objectives, retention, methodology, seminars, and reinforcement. These words are meaningful to teachers, but they may be no more than gobbledygook to students.

No wonder students throw up their hands in disgust and complain, "I just don't get what she's trying to get across. She says stuff that I don't understand!"

You are absolutely right to be flabbergasted and confounded! Students and teachers cannot communicate if both do not know the meaning of the words, signs, or symbols being used. New terminology and unfamiliar concepts are roadblocks to learning. Language is a bridge that must be constantly kept in repair if much traveling is to be done.

Teachers are usually blamed for this semantics barrier, although students use terminology unique to their generation and peer groups as well. The real strategy here is to ask questions, insist on clear directions, and demand to know the meaning of words—not just dictionary definitions, but the teacher's connotations too. Speaking out, asking the right questions at the right time is not only a student's responsibility, but also an important but neglected *right* that students do not exercise often enough.

Feedback

How often have you heard a teacher ask: "Now, are there any questions?" She is looking for some kind of feedback or response from you to see if you understood what she said.

Teachers evaluate your feedback when you turn in your answers to a quiz, a homework assignment, or a final examination. They also get feedback from your book reports, science projects, and your oral participation in group activities.

Feedback is the give-and-take between teacher and student in class. Without feedback, you can never be certain whether the person you are talking to understands your thoughts and ideas. Without constant feedback, the teacher can merely appear to be teaching; students can merely appear to be sitting quietly in class, learning. In reality, they may be faking each other out all together!

A communication problem arises when a student is frequently absent. A chronically truant student takes himself out of the communication process as well as the educational environment. As a result, he is unable to establish rapport with anyone, or maintain a working relationship with his teachers, or feel positive about attending school. He simply feels frustrated, alienated, confused, and alone.

Status Differences

The status of the teacher as an authority figure can become a communication problem when it interferes with the student's ability to learn. Like others, you may feel inferior or subordinate sitting in class watching the teacher give directions. Many students feel uncomfortable talking with their teachers because of peer pressure and lack of self-confidence. Some would much rather chat with friends than ask the teacher how to figure out a difficult problem. Don't fall into this No-Win Situation, because it only leads to an increase in the noise level of your class, and a decrease in the tolerance level of your teacher.

Students and teachers must learn to listen more carefully to one another. Effective two-way communication can occur only when one person speaks and the other person listens and when both understand the denotative and connotative meanings of the words, signs, and symbols expressed in their messages.

In other words, both students and teachers need to share in the exchange of ideas and to be responsible for the understanding that takes place. That does not mean that you must agree with everything that is said. But it does mean that you must be able to accept new ideas that are important and meaningful, even if those ideas come from teachers who are sometimes quite difficult.

CHAPTER ◇ 9

Watch Your Language

Don't most teachers pay particular attention to the way you write reports and essays, spell words, give speeches, and express yourself generally? Well then, give a little more thought to the way you use words and say what is on your mind.

Coping with difficult teachers is never easy, but it is never impossible either. You need a lot of determination and some effective communication strategies to keep your working relationships with them intact.

Teachers, more than most people, are extremely sensitive to the way you express your feelings and ideas. So the words you use and the way you speak can either get you in trouble or help you take charge of a conversation, conflict, or relationship.

Poor communication habits such as telling lies, using vulgar words, and making rude gestures should be avoided. Why? Because teachers, parents, and even your friends tend to react negatively when you swear or make embarrassing remarks. Poor speaking habits are often at the root of poor relationships. Teachers are twice as difficult to deal with when you are not in full command of your communication skills.

You *can* improve those skills. First, listen carefully to the teacher's pattern of speech, to what she says and how she says it. Next, be aware of her attitudes and the words she uses to express her feelings along with her use of facial expressions and gestures to get her point across. These are the words, signals, and signs *she* understands best! Don't imitate her actions and words; use paraphrases. Communicate with her by restating what she said, using some of your own words as well as some of hers. That way you will be on her wavelength and you will be more successful in answering questions, in justifying your actions, or in simply responding thoughtfully with your own ideas.

This communication strategy will help you take charge in two important ways. You will have proven that you were listening to what she said and that you understood the point she was trying to make.

Begin by asking: "Do you mean that..." and then rephrase her statement. Now you have made a verbal mirror of her thoughts and you have asked if it is accurate. One of two things will happen: The teacher will smile, look impressed, and be more receptive and friendly, or at least less antagonistic; or she will pause and become a little defensive while at the same time choosing her words with greater care. Either way, *you win!* You took charge and responded in a neutral manner, and at the same time you avoided any cause for her to create a No-Win Situation.

Such Language

Language can be nonsense turned into reason and logic. We speak, but we don't always say what we truly mean.

Neither do teachers! Often it is difficult to find the words that make sense not only to us but to others, and when we don't find the right words we blame others for not understanding what we want them to understand. Likewise, there are some very common "school phrases," questions and expressions on which students and teachers depend too much, language that grows out of vague thoughts and is heard as reasonably intelligent statements but misinterpreted nonetheless.

Thus, what is said is not always what is meant. In school, you must do more than just listen to get the full meaning. Do these statements hide your meanings?

STUDENTS' ROUNDABOUT PHRASES

What They Say	What They Mean
"May I go to the bathroom?"	"I need to get out of this room for a few minutes."
"May I sharpen my pencil?"	"I need to get up, stretch, sharpen my pencil, and walk around a bit."
"I always forget to bring my books and homework to school."	"I'm still immature, irresponsible, and I really can't remember to bring my school supplies— honest!"
"You always give us too much work!"	"I have never been able to finish that much work because I'm a slow worker. But give me enough time and I can finish and get an A."
"Why do you always pick on me?"	"You don't yell at other students as much as you yell at me, it seems. Why do you always yell at me, anyway?"
"Just sit down and be quiet."	"I'm having a difficult time coping with you, so give me a break!"

TEACHERS' ROUNDABOUT PHRASES

What They Say	What They Mean
"Are there any questions?"	"Tell me if you understood what I just said to you."
"Shape up or ship out!"	"Settle down, be quiet, or you will be in trouble."
"What in the world is this?"	"Your assignment is illegible, hard to read, or not what I expected you to hand in."
"Can't you do anything without constantly asking questions?"	"I am becoming annoyed and I wish you were smart enought to figure it out on your own."
"You *have* been warned! Now, do you want to be put on detention?"	"I have reprimanded you again and again for not following directions. Are you ready to pay the consequences for ignoring my warnings?"

Do you like to watch television or listen to music? Do you sing along with your favorite rock star? Or do you like to imitate the voice patterns and mannerisms of a comedian? Well, we all like to imitate. Students, more than most, like to pretend, model, and they enjoy listening to what they like.

Consciously or not, students have an innate ability to imitate the sounds and actions of people with whom they are in constant contact. Teachers, for example. You tend to pick up the idiosyncrasies, mannerisms, and pet phrases used by teachers in each of your classes.

Unfortunately, students, who are experts in imitating others, have no role model to pattern their listening habits after. They have never seen anyone in school, at home, or on television sit and listen attentively for six or seven hours a day, five days a week.

Student watch teachers. Teachers talk and talk and talk. So students pattern their communication habits by imitating their talk, talk, talk behavior just as they are used to imitating their favorite comedian, rock singer, or movie star. Furthermore, they watch their parents, who never sit and take notes, who never raise their hand to speak. Parents seem to talk more and listen less. What are students to learn from all this? That it is natural to talk about whatever comes to mind, whatever is interesting at the time, and to ignore everything else.

On the other hand, you may sit in class, look right at the teacher, and not hear a single word he is saying. It is possible for you to daydream and to hear his words without understanding what he is telling the class. This is called *passive listening*. Sounds go in one ear and out the other without checking in with the brain. Information never gets processed, analyzed, or remembered. For this reason, you need to write notes to remind yourself what you heard. This is especially helpful in classes that are always being interrupted by messages on the intercom system, by bells ringing, or by other extraneous noises that get in the way of your ability to concentrate.

Active listening is when you take good notes, volunteer answers, and ask thoughtful questions in class. Your brain sits up and takes notice, sorting, decoding, and storing information for future reference. This kind of listening takes a lot more energy. You are actively participating in the exchange of ideas. In short, you are learning to manipulate the language so that what was once nonsense turns into something reasonable, logical, and meaningful.

Most teachers expect students to listen during class

discussions. So improving your listening skills may keep you out of trouble with difficult teachers. Remember the last time one of them asked; "Well, why weren't you listening while I was explaining that assignment? Don't you ever listen?"

Improving your listening skills is not as easy as it may sound. You will need the teacher's help. In fact, it should be the teacher's responsibility as well as yours to increase your ability to concentrate and to hear what is important. Teachers can help by making their students aware of important terminology to listen for that is peculiar to the subject and grade level being taught; teaching styles, habits, and mannerisms; and other communication skills that will enhance the students' ability to learn in each teacher's classroom environment.

As a student, you need to learn to "read" the teacher's moods and feelings and anticipate her teaching habits. Find out how all of these affect your grade and your behavior toward her. Find out what is the most important information for you to concentrate on during class.

In every classroom, teacher and student have an obligation to one another to maintain a good working relationship and to keep the communication channels open, friendly, and positive.

MANAGING SCHOOL QUESTIONS

Just as teachers expect you to listen during class discussions, they also expect you to answer questions about facts and ideas mentioned in that discussion. It seems that easy teachers ask easy questions whereas difficult teachers ask impossible questions. So asking and answering questions is an essential part of trying to get along with whatever kind of teacher you have. The best strategy for that is knowing what kinds of questions there are and what to do about them.

Basically, questions are of two general types. Some are positive and help you and the teacher explore information that is being discussed in class. Others are posed in a negative manner, not for the purpose of learning but for the purpose of damaging someone's self-image.

Manageable Questions

Some questions are not really questions at all. "What's up? How are you? What are you doing after school?" You need only reply with a smile, "Not much," or "Fine" as brief acknowledgment. Such questions are not meant to test your IQ nor to put you on the spot or tease you. They are meant to open up a conversation or simply to acknowledge that someone other than yourself is present. These questions are easily manageable because you respond with an appropriate answer and feel assured that you have said the right thing.

Other kinds of manageable questions are more thought-provoking and more challenging, with a more specific purpose. Model teachers do ask difficult questions but in such a way that you can manage them. They encourage you to "guess" or to "tell what you know." Good teachers know how to challenge your thinking skills without putting you on the spot. Difficult teachers, on the other hand, don't!

Still other manageable questions you must pose to the teacher, asking for further instructions or more detailed information. "What did I do wrong in this problem?" or "How can the word *rose* be a noun, a verb, *and* an adjective?"

At first the teacher's answer may make no sense. But

you will also find that there are more manageable questions when talking with good teachers than with difficult teachers.

Generally, model teachers answer your questions in a positive, helpful manner, not only because that is their job, but also because they enjoy sharing knowledge and helping their students grow in understanding. If you are used to arguing or nagging teachers, your interactions with them may not be filled with directions and information, but rather with reprimands and unfriendly remarks.

There are three kinds of manageable questions of which you should be aware. The first are *open-ended questions*. These are questions teachers ask students in order to gain feedback. They require the student to explain his answer or to back up his words with some rationale. So you can't just mumble, "Yes, that's right" or "No, that's wrong."

These questions are easy to identify. They usually begin with, "Why do you think?..." How do you feel?..." or "What are the major differences between?..."

The second kind are *leading questions*. Teachers expect you to give a specific answer or response, replying with facts covered in class or in a chapter reading. These are difficult questions asked more often by difficult teachers, and are especially difficult if you haven't done your homework.

Examples of these questions include: "What was the surprise ending in this story?" What molecules combine to make water?" "Exactly what is the Bill of Rights?" Such questions are frequently followed by a *follow-up question*. "What else can you add?" or "How does this tie in with what we have just discussed?"

Finally, there are the *directive questions*. Teachers ask these questions when they want to keep everyone's attention focused on the main point of the lesson or discussion.

For instance, teachers often ask: "All that may be true, but what started it in the first place? How did this all come about?" or "Based on what we have been saying, how can this author make such a statement?"

As you can see, these questions are not intended to trick you, embarrass you, or put you on the spot. They are types of questions that are asked to help you further develop interest and information in a particular topic or subject matter.

Unmanageable Questions

Other questions that are asked in class are not manageable because they are not posed in a friendly manner, nor is their purpose to enlighten or educate. Instead, these questions are insulting, demeaning, and from them grow classroom unrest, hostility, tension, and conflict. These questions help only to build barriers to communication. They are indirectly a form of insult or accusation made to intimidate or embarrass.

Put-down questions are used all too often by both teacher and student to antagonize and belittle. They are the "Didn't-I-tell-you-so" questions used in a derogatory manner, usually in the heat of a conflict.

The teacher snaps at a student: "Didn't I tell everyone that answer just two seconds ago? Why can't you pay attention like everyone else?" Or students may moan: "Don't you think that's quite a lot of work for us to do in one period? Aren't you expecting too much of us?" Such insinuations are meant to put others on the spot or on the defensive. They are unmanageable questions because no matter what the response is, it's the wrong one. It is one that will stoke the fires of discontent, create fertile ground for No-Win Situations, and cause animosity between student and teacher. That is the intent of unmanageable questions: to put people further apart.

Trick questions are also unmanageable because of the way they are designed. They usually have vague terminology, hidden meanings, or a deceptive purpose. These are the kind of questions that many difficult teachers utilize most often, making learning a very distasteful experience.

Brain teasers, although they too are *trick questions*, nevertheless are seen by students as a challenge to match wits, not to spite or give insult. These are usually questions of pure logic, based in part on semantics, or founded on trivia. Such questions may be unmanageable, but the outcome is fun, not conflict.

No matter what kind of teacher you are dealing with, no matter what kind of question is being asked, reach out with confidence.

RULE 16. BE CONFIDENT, SHOW GOODWILL AND KINDNESS TOWARD DIFFICULT TEACHERS, AND YOU AND THEY WILL SOON BECOME FRIENDS.

CHAPTER 10

By the Rules

Never have so many rules been imposed on so many people, in all of history, as in the last quarter of the twentieth century. Multitudes of national and state laws regulate how we do business with one another, how we drive vehicles on the streets, and how we act and speak to one another in public and private. There are laws that impose state taxes, city taxes, and county fees. There are community ordinances, decrees, and proclamations that govern the sale and use of land as well as personal property. And there are rules and codes of conduct that regulate our behavior, many of them firmly rooted in tradition, others declared by Supreme Court decisions. Some are revised; some go unchallenged. But people, whether they agree or disagree, are expected to obey them. School policy and classroom rules are no different.

Whether we like obeying rules or not is not at issue here. What is important is the consequences of those rules. Positive consequences are praise, good grades, and honors at the time of graduation. Negative consequences include being chastised or given detention, suspension, or in the extreme form, expulsion. The implementation of these consquences is often justified by the ever-popular euphemism, "teaching a lesson," changing undesirable social behavior into more appropriate conformity.

Rules do provide a working contract within a working relationship, however. When all parties agree to a set of rules, contentment and harmony abound. Otherwise, disagreement and conflict generated by mixed emotions lead to confusion and chaos. This is especially true in school.

In a classroom, rules define limits of student conduct and expectations. If both teacher and students agree to them, chances are that an enjoyable, friendly atmosphere will be created, one conducive to a quality education. However, if teachers impose unfair rules or students consistently disobey school policies, the working contract quickly breaks down, and efforts to share information become difficult if not impossible.

You may feel that some classroom rules are too limiting, too stringent. You may also think that some are enforced in a helter-skelter fashion, and thus breaking those rules or bucking the system becomes your top priority, if only to disrupt the class. If you are the type of student who cannot follow any rules imposed by any teacher, you may have a very serious, chronic school problem.

But, like most problems, you can cope with this one because it has alternatives to be considered. For instance, if you cannot go by school rules, why not adopt those you have read in this book. Make them a permanent part of your life-style. Why? Because they are less restrictive, perhaps more meaningful, and best of all, you are in complete control because they are self-imposed.

PERSONAL RULES

1. Change your behavior. Then adjust to the problems of daily school life with confidence and a take-charge attitude.
2. Nobody needs to feel like a failure. There are so many alternatives and effective strategies to rely on when coping with difficult people. Whenever possible, find the Win-Win Situation.
3. Fight frustration by staying in control and planning ahead. Take charge of every school situation by looking for better alternatives.
4. Be calm in a crisis. Bring conflicts under control by dispelling negative feelings with a friendly smile and by communicating your concerns objectively.
5. Whenever you cope with mixed emotions, first count up all the good things that happen to you and contemplate the nature of *change*.
6. Be willing to give as much as you take from any relationship and you will be better able to cope with difficult people.
7. Play it smart! Handle school conflicts before they handle you.
8. Find the courage to meet life on its own terms. Be responsible and mature no matter what situation you find yourself in.
9. Your problems are already half solved once you fully understand them.
10. Disarm the negativism of others by showing goodwill toward them. You can produce a positive effect on those who care about you.
11. Getting the most out of education and life is

knowing that there is a challenge to be met.

12. Your challenge is not to eliminate the anger in others; rather it is to control your own reactions.

13. If people sense that you have a high opinion of yourself, they will also share that opinion.

14. Think first, then respond to people in a positive, friendly way.

15. Find your goal in life, but never make unrealistic demands on yourself.

16. Be confident, show goodwill and kindness toward difficult teachers, and you and they will soon become friends.

17. Always be a friend to yourself. If you cannot always follow this rule then at the very least say this, "No matter what anyone does or says to me, *I am still a worthwhile person!*"

Index